WALK

the

Eastern
Hadrianic Way

Ravenglass
to Ambleside

Being a Guide to the Roman Byways from Ravenglass to
Ambleside, including some new discoveries along the way.

36 kilometres in distance, two thousand years in time
A walk, not for the faint-hearted.

*"You will be walking in Roman footsteps in one of the
remotest locations of the Western Roman Empire.
It's well worth the effort."*

Author

CLIFFORD JONES, BA HONS

First published 2009

Published by: Buckland Jones Archaeological Press

10 9 8 7 6 5 4 3 2 1

The right of Clifford Jones to be identified as the author of this work has been asserted in accordance with the Copyrights, Designs and Patents Act 1988.

ISBN 978-0-9562229-0-9

Distributed by: Striding Edge Limited, Crag House Farm, Wasdale, Cumbria CA19 1UT, ENGLAND
Tel: +44 (0)19467 26090 ~ Fax: +44 (0)19467 26050

Typesetting and origination by trevor@epic-gb.com
Printed in the UK by Ashford Colour Press Ltd, Gosport, Hants

Contents

A Warning Note from the Author

The author is not noted for any agreement with the 'Nanny State', considering personal common sense and responsibility to be a better guide.

However, in this instance, the author will bring to the attention of the walker (who no doubt will have looked at their maps in preparation) a large expanse from Boot to Little Langdale with virtually not a living soul in it.

It's a magnificent piece of North Britain that inspires the soul of those that walk it.

But, can also kill.

The author suggests that attempting Hardknott and Wrynose Pass in winter is an unacceptable risk to life and limb and especially to those who have to pick up your pieces afterwards.

The gates at the passes are closed, not out of a desire for neatness, and the notices regarding closure due to weather conditions do not just apply to motorists.

At any other time, check the weather report, take your time and enjoy this magnificent route; make sure someone knows when you traverse the passes; intended destination and when completed confirm that you have done so.

You will get wet. Prepare accordingly.

ALWAYS MAKE A CONTRIBUTION to
Wasdale & Langdale Mountain Rescue Teams
COLLECTION TINS ARE ALONG THE ROUTE

or

make a regular donation

www.wasdale.mountain.rescue.org.uk

The LMRT Treasurer

The Secretary, LAMRT, Lowfold Base, Lake Road, Ambleside, Cumbria LA22 0DN

...for they will be the people giving of their free time, in extreme circumstances, to come to your rescue.

Children and Dogs

There is good reason to consider that parts of this route are extremely strenuous – which no doubt the young will thoroughly enjoy and leave everyone else standing. This is an adventure – kids and canines like real challenges. This is one.

However, the ever-present motor car is a hazard; there are precipitous situations in the most unexpected and publicly used places and the days are long and can (if the weather is against you) be debilitating. The passes in particular are barren spots when the rain begins to fall.

So there is need for very close supervision at all times.

NOTE

It is the responsibility of the walker to carry a suitable map and compass and know how to use them.

Only contact the Mountain Rescue in a genuine emergency. Getting lost is not in itself an emergency. Ringing up the rescue services for directions only hinders their efforts and stretches volunteer resources.

It is unlikely that your mobile phone will work in the upper parts of Eskdale and Wrynose Pass.

The Roman road through Wrynose is on the opposite side of the river and therefore remote from human intervention.

Always carry a whistle and torch and if walking alone keep to the present road or well-trodden track throughout this walk.

Pack plenty of common sense in the back pack.

Here follows PRACTICAL SAFETY INFORMATION, so placed to find easily when you (hopefully) will not need it.

DON'T CALL
THE MOUNTAIN RESCUE
FOR DIRECTIONS.
YOU ARE RISKING
ANOTHER'S LIFE

Before you start every day check
LDNP Weatherline
0870 055 0575

EMERGENCY INFORMATION

By: Mr. Mike Greene FRCS FFAEM
Consultant Accident & Emergency Medicine
Wasdale & Langdale Mountain Rescue Teams

WHAT TO DO IF A WALKER OR CLIMBER IS INJURED

Ensure your own safety and that of the casualty from a further fall or injury.
Follow the A-I of Mountain First Aid.
Make the casualty as comfortable as possible and provide shelter from the elements. All injured and immobile casualties are at risk of hypothermia.
Ensure the safety of the rest of the party.
Call for help by attracting the attention of others on the fells. Use the international distress signal of a series of six blasts of a whistle or flashes of a torch to attract attention.
Send for help. Send two people if possible. Write down a message giving the exact location, time of accident, nature of injuries and other details as known. Have one person stay with the casualty.
Dial 999 and ask for Police and Mountain Rescue.

THIS IS VERY IMPORTANT

STAY BY THE PHONE UNLESS INSTRUCTED TO DO OTHERWISE.
IF USING A MOBILE PHONE LEAVE IT SWITCHED ON AND STAY IN THE POSITION IN WHICH YOU HAVE A SIGNAL

A-I of Mountain First Aid

A – Assess the accident site.
Assess the safety of the casualty, other party members and yourself.
Assess the cause of the accident – it will provide clues to the injuries sustained.

A – Approach with care.
Do not cause a second accident.

A – Airway.
Ask the patient a question. A casualty who can talk has an open airway. If they are not responsive an airway problem can be anticipated. LOOK, LISTEN & FEEL for air movement at the mouth.
If this is not present remove any obvious vomit or foreign material from the mouth using a finger. The tongue can be lifted from the back of the mouth using a jaw lift or thrust manoeuvre. Avoid moving the neck of an unconscious injured climber. The cervical spine should be held still by another helper and then immobilised before they are transported to prevent injury to the spinal cord.

B – Breathing.
LOOK & FEEL for movements of the chest wall.
The chest should move symmetrically and the normal rate of breathing is 12 – 16 breaths per minute. Fast or slow rates should alert you to a potentially serious problem that will prompt a high degree of urgency for rescue.

C – Circulation.
Blood loss may be obvious from a wound or open fracture. In general applying direct pressure and elevating the limb if this is possible should control external bleeding. Internal bleeding into the chest or abdomen may be expected from the mechanism of accident and the casualty's physical condition. Look for signs of severe blood loss – a fast pulse >100 per minute, rapid breathing, pallor, sweaty skin and anxiety or loss of consciousness. These signs require a high degree of urgency in rescue.

D – Disability.
This really means conscious level. Is the casualty Alert and can answer

all your questions, only responds to Verbal commands, worse only to Pain or are they Unresponsive? (A.V.P.U. score) This information will be helpful to the rescue team in assessing the urgency of the situation. Reassess the conscious level of a casualty with a head injury at regular intervals and report changes to the team.

E – Exposure to the elements.

Any mountain casualty is at risk of rapid cooling and hypothermia as are the accompanying party and rescuers.

Arrange shelter and insulation from the ground as soon as possible to prevent the condition from becoming worse.

F – Fractures.

LOOK & FEEL for fractures. These are common in mountaineering accidents. Look in particular for suspected fractures of the spine where inappropriate movement may cause further damage, rib fractures which may have injured the lungs and pelvic fractures which can bleed heavily. Immobilise and splint a fractured limb. Provide suitable pain relief if possible.

G & H – Get Help.

If you use a cell phone stay where you are and DO NOT TURN IT OFF – the rescue team will want to talk to you for more information after you have dialled 999 and spoken to the police. The number of casualties and an assessment of injuries.

I – I hope you never have to use this information!

Good Luck.
By Mr. Mike Greene FRCS FFAEM
Consultant Accident & Emergency Medicine
Wasdale Mountain Rescue Team

What To Do if You are Lost on the Fells

STOP AND THINK

Get your party into shelter and assess your situation.

Decide are you in real danger or just lost?

Think back to what you have been doing.

What was your last definite known location, e.g. summit of a mountain?

What type of terrain have you been walking on? Which direction have you been walking (you need a compass to work this out!)? For how long have you been walking? Use your navigation skills to work out an estimated position.

Can you now retrace your steps to a known position of safety and start again?

Can you use the estimated position to travel on safely and collect more navigational clues until you get a definite fix of your position and can walk out safely?

Consider whether you have the equipment to navigate off the fell safety, e.g. map, compass, torch.

Is the party able to finish the journey safely?

What would be the consequence of a night out on the fells – unpleasant or really dangerous? If really trapped on the mountain seek shelter and use your emergency equipment to keep the party warm and a whistle and torch to attach attention.

If there is real danger to the party or individuals call for help using a mobile phone if it will work!

REMEMBER THE BEST WAY TO AVOID GETTING LOST IS TO LEARN HOW TO NAVIGATE PROPERLY, TO PRACTISE IN ALL WEATHERS AND ALWAYS LEAVE A ROUTE CARD WITH SOMEONE RESPONSIBLE.

Introduction

This is a Grand Walk

This is a walk, not for the faint-hearted.

On the map it may not be far; it does not constitute a long-distance walk, but it is one of the hardest. Distance is not measured in miles, it should be measured in effort and personal experience. Walking over Hardknott and Wrynose is an experience.

But do not be discouraged by sensible cautionary advice.

You are truly walking in Roman footsteps in one of the remotest locations of the western empire. The warning notes are those the author trusts – enough to make the walker plan well ahead and thoroughly enjoy the route.

So, do not be alarmed, this is a walk of remarkable contrasts, of coastal plain, river valleys and high mountains and the intimacy and fervour of the central lakes. The walker can dip feet in water at both ends; enjoy good hospitality and magnificent scenery along the way.

Plenty of physical Roman remains to keep the mind focussed on the archaeology of the route and the opportunity to have an opinion. If

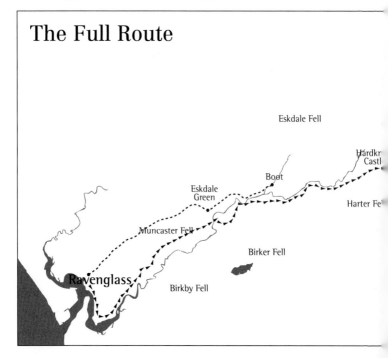

The Full Route

you note something you think is worthy of going in the next edition, let the author know. This guide will never be a finished piece; there will always be a need for new discoveries to be noted. It, at the least, provides a wall for further canvasses to be hung on.

Much historical research is currently being carried out at Muncaster Castle and in Eskdale by the Eskdale Historical Society and they deserve your support. See Listings for details.

The Romans did not just arrive on the shore at Ravenglass and set up their imperial structures overnight; like all long-term projects, things take time. But one thing is certain, the Romans understood the terrain well, they were fully aware of the mineral contents of the fells, the timber and the locals that inhabited it.

This is equally the case with Galava (Ambleside), nestled below fells on every side. The Romans must have known their neighbours pretty well, both to establish a base and then enhance their presence; although there is evidence that all was not always well with the locals at Galava, but more on that anon.

Exploiting the natural environment and taming it is difficult in the Western Fells; in fact the Romans exploited it very well, but never really tamed it – roads were thrust west to east as part of the need for a military back up for troop movements further North in Britain and for

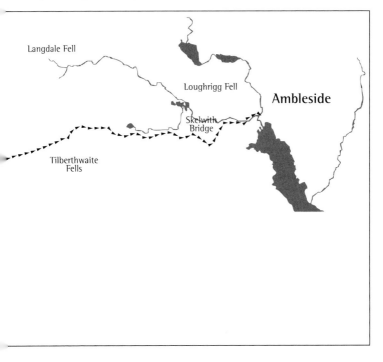

basic administrative links. However, it will be clear to the walker that these roads would be death traps if the natives decided to be less than friendly, with the opportunity for rock hurling competitions along the way. The roads are a whisper on the landscape, a slender strand of Imperial power, un-noticed by a greater power, that of nature. They may not feel so underfoot, but the roads cannot dominate the scene and the Romans knew this as well as we.

Step off the track and you are in an environment that is in as wild a condition as it was two thousand years ago. It has been tweaked and nudged along the way, but for the most part it is little changed. The odd hole for mining and quarrying; the spot of river valley released by the river from its grip, providing man with land for crops; otherwise it is what it will always be – wilderness.

The walker will enjoy the delights of Ravenglass, the way along the Esk and up into the heart of Eskdale. The dale embraces the traveller, even on a wet day. The way is good underfoot, muddy in places, but a walker cannot consider the job done without some evidence of effort.

Boot offers excellent respite and some really superb excursions, so the walker may wish to stay awhile longer than the prescribed timescale and the author offers some excellent reasons for dallying, so read on.

Hardknott to Wrynose is spectacular, tough, but worth every bit of effort. The walker can genuinely feel at one with the surroundings, especially if Hardknott is tackled early in the morning. Listen for the tramp of steadily marching feet, the muffled clatter of steel on steel. The past is with you all the way and as the descent towards Wrynose begins you will begin to sense the way as well as see it, for the present road diverts from the Roman one for the journey through Wrynose. By then the walker is attuned with the past, can sense a presence in every breath. When the wind howls and the rain passes by horizontally the grimness is put aside by the knowledge that feet have trod in equal measure every step and weathered the same storm and come through having been the better for it.

The walker can only experience the passes by walking them; the past is there and there is no other way of experiencing the sheer presence and force of man trying to impose a way across the landscape and for all the technology and effort only managing to wind his way as nature demands. The motorist is cocooned from this and only sees a view.

The great descent towards Little Langdale (with the Three Shires pub a worthy and much deserved goal) is a marked contrast; the walker will become aware of fussy little fields and intimate landscapes on the way through to Skelwith Bridge. A world away from the ruggedness of the heights the walker has struggled over. The sense of change of scale and terrain is palpable, a gentleness and modernity now prevails, things become pretty and charming, intimate and within the scope of an ordinary camera lens. The presence of man's hewn effort brings the walker back from the past.

Galava sits in a very magnificent location overlooking Windermere and is utterly compromised as a military base as a result of it. Instead of looking down on the lake, it's nearly in it; with good evidence that it had the water lapping on two sides in the not-too-distant past. It seems, whilst constructed for military purposes, the administration of the area and trade pre-occupied the fort's career. The transportation of goods by water makes perfect sense and the location allows for observation of craft movements at the north end of the lake. Archaeologists have long wondered about a fort at the other end of Windermere; please give us time, we will get around to it in time and the present mere is a shadow of its former self, so the location of such a fort is not as clear cut as previously perceived.

You are ground breaking. Not many walk this way; the Hardknott to Fold End section has become the land of the motor car. Let the walker recapture it. Be part of that campaign.

Maps

Ordnance Survey Outdoor Leisure 6 & 7, 1:25000, cover the route in full. Make sure they have a suitable waterproof cover!

Some Basics

The author does not provide full maps in the guide because the author knows that the walker will make proper provision in this respect. As ever the author also expects the walker to get lost, it's part of the process of discovery.

"Just be careful how you go about it and think before you step."

It is the responsibility of the walker to understand how to use the grid co-ordinates of a map.

"A contour line looks easy on paper but can be a bucket of sweat in the flesh." Author

Walking in the Roman Army's Footsteps

Getting Started

Basic Principles

Good worn-in boots

To enjoy a good walk, have the right boots; this is a tough expedition taking approximately five or six days and a comfortable pair of boots is essential. A mixture of shingle, mud, granite and tarmac with a good few gallons of water thrown in will test even a good pair. So be prepared.

The Roman equivalent of the lightweight walking shoe or boot is the 'Caligae' – an apparently flimsy leather sandal, not offering much in the way of protection from the elements. However the design allowed for the foot to be well ventilated cutting down on the chance of blisters developing. Fitted with studs for grip and imposing severe injury on fallen enemy forces and useful for trampling new road surfaces alike the flimsiness belies this extremely tough design.

The author has recently witnessed someone wearing the modern equivalent and they work even in the toughest conditions; what is required is a toughened foot, which takes about a year of wandering around in bare feet to get into perfect condition.

Waterproofs: An Essential

West Cumbria can be a glorious spot on a good day, but the weather can be extremely inclement, especially on exposed sections, such as beaches or cliff tops. A good quality set of lightweight waterproofs, including over-trousers, is a must.

The Roman equivalent was the 'sagum', a thick woollen cloak. Service on the Hadrianic Wall was severe enough for the Romans to adopt a version of local cloak with hood and the Vindolanda tablets identify a constant need for more socks and underwear, suggesting a cold posting!

The sagum has the advantage of being a multi-purpose article; especially useful as a towel.

You will need a towel on this trip and one packed at the top of the back pack, next to the dry socks for immediate use. There are rivers and becks to cross.

DON'T FORGET THE MIDGE SPRAY!

No Roman equivalent other than twenty year-old fish sauce on the breath!

Bait: An Army marches on its stomach

This route has very limited opportunity for provisioning, which means stocking up or making arrangements with your hotel or guest house in advance. There is a small shop at Ravenglass, and another at Eskdale Green which the author encourages the walker to use whenever possible. Skelwith Fold caravan site has a shop.

The Romans set up forts and milecastles as part of a defensive strategy, but also because the army understood that the men needed to rest at regular intervals. The walker should take note of this. There is a potential site for a half-way house in Wrynose Pass.

The Roman military understood dry rations but when in a fort, or on frontier duty, the basic healthy diet would be a grain ration 1-1½kg per day (2-3lb) which for the most part would be ground for bread-making. Bread ovens are prevalent all over Roman military establishments, often used to keep parts of forts warm in winter. At Housesteads there are bread ovens near the latrines, useful to stop the occupants freezing in winter!

The archaeological excavations at Hardknott have not found the latrines yet, but the author suspects that there will be bread ovens nearby. Archaeological remains identify the troops had frying pans, allowing for a filling and quick and easy meal in the field, or, using a stew pot, produce a good meaty dinner – keeping the belly full and warding off the cold. Fresh vegetables complemented this diet and the soldier could further supplement this by popping into the local vicus to one of the bars, or shops, for a quick wine and dormouse on a stick. Even at Hardknott there appears to have been a thriving settlement; in fact the difficulty of the location probably meant a vicus was encouraged, to provide some relief from the location. The author anticipates lamb being on the menu.

Observe & Record

As the author stresses, you the walker may notice something that he and his fellow archaeologists have missed. In fact you are sure to see something new, because that is the way of things; the author has walked past many features, sometimes for years without noticing what is under his nose. All it takes, in some instances, is the time of day, the angle of the sun and being in the right place. And that will vary by the moment.

The idea of this guide is for the walker to explore and not be fooled by us so-called specialists and experts.

Take a photo, make a note and let the author know. Every bit of information helps put the picture together.

Observe and learn your territory.

He sought to make himself acquainted with the province and known to the army.

Tacitus: Agricola
Trans. A J Church & W J Brodribb, London: Macmillan, 1877

Common Sense

Please keep to paths and keep erosion down and remember that agriculture plays an enormous part in the Cumbrian economy. So close gates after you.

On this walk extreme care is needed beyond the gates to Hardknott Pass and Wrynose. Consider carefully before proceeding and check weather forecasts. One option for the walk through Wrynose is not along the present road and communications can be extremely poor. Be sure, be safe.

Plan ahead, ring establishments to check opening times, as they will vary with the seasons.

Open Mind

Explore your senses.

The walk is deliberately started at Ravenglass, because Ravenglass is an acknowledged Roman harbour and a staging post for onward journeys northward. It was chosen because of its fresh water supplies.

It is good to be able to offer a walk involving Roman Britain with physical remains (the Roman Bath House at Ravenglass, the Tile Kilns of Eskdale; Hardknott Fort; Galava Fort; and the Roman road itself). All encourage the walker on the bleakest of days.

Slowly, as the walker progresses along the way, the process of observing and understanding the landscape and making decisions and theorems of their own as to where the frontier lies, begins.

A rise in the ground level, a river to cross, a change in the coastline, an old beach inland, a dried up river course.

Why is that field that shape?

Why is that grass greener and longer than the rest?

Why doesn't that crop grow well just in that one patch?

Why does that stream go at right angles?

These are all clues which the walker can consider, record and enjoy the process of finding.

Wherever practicable, the walker is walking in the Roman Army's footsteps. This is a long-lost route, which, by the walking, will come back to life.

You are the eyes and sensations of the past. Meet the past with eyes and senses. Record as you go.

This route over the mountains was undoubtedly no less a slog for the Romans as it is for us. The rain and wind are eternal features; the sense of isolation and the shadow of the mountains all add to a sense of expectation; as every brow is met the wish is for it to be the summit. The relief, when it is, is palpable.

Enjoy.

Research

The route of the Roman road through Eskdale has been the source of academic debate for over 150 years. The author, having walked the lands of Eskdale for over twenty years, is not entering the fray to establish its whereabouts. There are several options. The main problem is that, contrary to popular belief, the construction of a Roman road does not follow a single civil construction pattern, varying as to location and need. Only if a datable item is found in the construction layer – for example pottery or coins – can an absolute date be considered for a road. Roman roads are a means of moving troops around. Commerce and the locations of production may well vary from the military need, so there could well be a series of multi-purposes trackways from the Roman period that are still in use since they departed. The sources of iron, water and clay are constants in the dale.

Therefore, the walker is as likely to find the road as those who have sought it for most of their working lives. In the case of the author he prefers to consider the water option for goods to and fro in the dale. There is more to the river Esk than meets the eye; it is a much gentler river during the last two hundred years.

In every case of a newly-found site under archaeological research the exact location has been excluded from this guide. This is to protect the archaeology from those seeking only personal material profit.

Please report any obvious human intervention or finds found as the result of erosion at known archaeological sites to:

English Heritage
North West Region
Canada House
3 Chepstow Street
Manchester
M1 5FW
Tel: 0161 242 1400

Where possible provide details of location including grid reference.

Lakeland colours.

Route Planning

The section from the gates of Hardknott Pass and Wrynose must be treated with considerable respect.

The walker may wish to dip in and out of this guide for weekend excursions; here are some basic facts to note:

Most importantly remember that the further into the remote areas you go for a day excursion, the more limited the options are for an easy return. Watch the time and allow more time than you think to get back.

Note that details of public transport are liable to seasonal change so check with service providers and the journey planner website or phone.

0871 200 22 33

Rail:

Lancaster – Barrow – Ravenglass – Carlisle: Monday to Saturday.
Carlisle to Whitehaven: every day (limited Sunday).
Services are operated by Northern Rail.

Windermere to London via Oxenholme: daily.
Services operated by First Transpennine Express.
Also Virgin connecting services.

Bus:

Carlisle to Whitehaven: daily (limited Sunday).
Carlisle to Ravenglass: one connecting service down coast, two back (requires changes).

Whitehaven to Ravenglass: daily but limited. (Sundays, a surprisingly useful service.)

Ambleside to Windermere: daily.
Great Langdale to Ambleside: Langdale Rambler (limited out of season).

http://www.traveline.info/index.htm
or 0871 200 22 33

Keywords: Traveline, Cumbria

DO CHECK IN ADVANCE REGARDING ALL SERVICES AND FACILITIES

Please Note
Bus stops are an uncommon sight in many areas. Take local advice and normally in very rural areas if a clear hand signal is given the bus will stop where it is safe to do so.

Where to Stay

The guide is broken into days all ending at points where there are accommodation options. But remember to book in advance and the further east on the route the walker goes the options become scarce, so good planning is a must.

Those taking their home in their pack, please ask before you pitch if not using recognised sites.

Traversing the Passes

There is no regular public transport over the passes. Mountain Goat and Lakes Super Tours operate a daily excursion from Windermere as part of a day tour. Details in the Listings section.

Hadrian's Wall Heritage Limited and The Ravenglass & Eskdale Railway run a combined rail, mini-bus and guided tour of Hardknott. Contact the RER for details. 01229 717171.

Stage One

Starting the walk at Ravenglass,
          or walking around it!

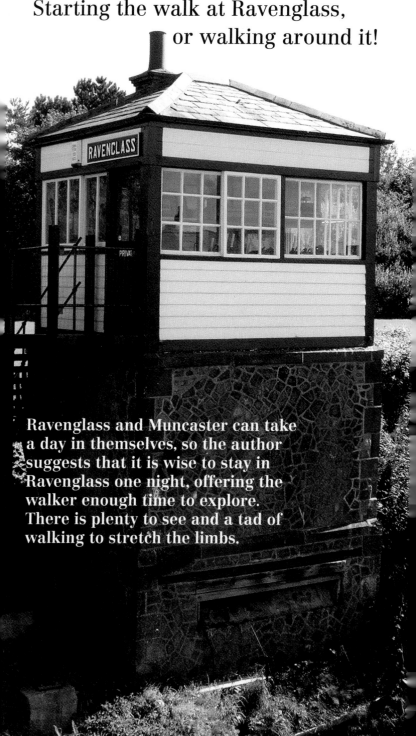

Ravenglass and Muncaster can take
a day in themselves, so the author
suggests that it is wise to stay in
Ravenglass one night, offering the
walker enough time to explore.
There is plenty to see and a tad of
walking to stretch the limbs.

STAGE 1

Arrival at Ravenglass.

Let the Train Take the Strain

The author fully promotes the use of public transport, which is vital for the long term future of West Cumbria and the rest of the nation to boot! Booking tickets in advance, by internet, is very good value; the walker can book to Ravenglass to start and return via Windermere station, which is the closest to the end of the walk. You can even book a through ticket to Dalegarth on the Ratty. Ravenglass can be reached from anywhere within mainland UK in a day, but the further south, or north, you are the earlier you will have to start. If you left St Ives, or Thurso, on the first train you will make it to Ravenglass on the very last train of the day – just! It is hoped that the rail timetable service will be extended to later arrivals and departures than the present and a service on Sundays is very much needed.

Arriving by rail at Ravenglass is simply the best way and if not, enjoy the bus ride down from Whitehaven. In both cases, the traveller will gain the sense of scale of the size of the barrier inland and the contrast with the coastal plain. It becomes clear to the expectant traveller how West Cumbria is a very long way from anywhere. Walkers arriving at Carlisle will step on to a train that will come as rather a shock to most; the mainline luxury and comfort vanishes and a rattling good journey down the West

STAGE 1

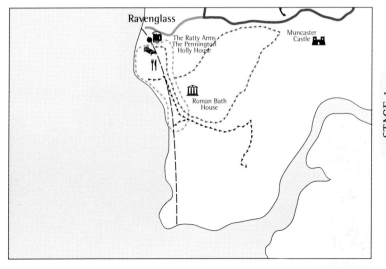

Cumbrian coast commences; trains are well frequented; there is often a spot of crack; the staff friendly (Northern Rail seems to have a knack of finding people with good sense and a smile), but most importantly the scenery is absorbing; open fields and countryside give way to the vanished world of steel; to Georgian ports; the nuclear industry and back to nature again; all bordered by the sea. That's what makes it unique. This is a remote world where the elements are obvious, people genuine and the welcome heartfelt.

Both means of transport bring you to Ravenglass station which is rather conveniently also the pub, and the author cannot think of a finer waiting room. The Ratty Arms is named after the Ravenglass & Eskdale Railway, the terminus of which is right next door to the Network Rail line. The 3ft-gauge La'al Ratty conveyed haematite for the iron producing furnaces flourishing along the Cumbrian coast in the late nineteenth century, now (half the track width) it provides a regular service that allows the explorer to visit Eskdale. The walker may wish to consider it a fast option to Dalegarth, Boot and Hardknott beyond if limited for time.

STAGE 1

Ravenglass station.

The Ratty Arms has a unique atmosphere; the ex Furness railway station building makes an unusually designed pub. It is not the only such re-use of station premises; it does, from time to time, have a feel of a station bar, people coming and going – transient, a pint snatched before rushing for a train; it is a 'local', the intrigue of day-to-day of life in Ravenglass; a place for joining in, making a point and taking a rebuttal on the chin; a place to listen, laugh and mull; a place to dine with friends. The din and crush can be too much, but the crackle of the fire on a winter night with a small cluster of regulars sheltering from inner winter darkness warms the soul. It is the taste of good beer, the meeting of friends on both sides of the bar. It is a place to belong.

The Ratty Arms is usually busy, especially on Friday and Saturday evenings, so if you intend to arrive and want to dine, book in advance. Details at the end of this guide.

Ravenglass village has a picture-postcard main street, courtesy of the efforts of the local residents who cannot be praised enough for their constant effort. The walker will notice the pinch points at either end, to hold cattle and sheep before being transhipped on to vessels, Ravenglass was a trading post long before the Romans and remaining in constant use until the eighteenth century when the ports of Whitehaven and Maryport, with their easier access to the sea, gave them prominence. There was a regular market at Ravenglass and a charter permitting trading dates back to 1208 (which is not just after twelve-o-clock), but this appears to only legitimise activity – and potentially tax it – that had been carried on long before the ink hit the velum. Nor is it clear that the market took place at the location that it is now associated with it in Main Street; it seems most unlikely that a market would take place on what then would still be an open site with craft beaching on the hard. More likely in the fields next to Walls Drive, near to the Bath House, effectively on top of the Roman vicus, where of course there would have been a market, suggesting a continuity of use. This location away from the shoreline provides some distance from uninvited guests arriving by sea, no doubt wishing to exchange blows for goods rather than coin.

The Pennington Hotel stands at the eastward end, and beyond that the Holly House that is a snug little spot with a good pint and a fine view.

Raids by sea would have been a threat along the coast, the most fearful of all being those kidnapping women and children for the slave trade. This may come as a surprise, but coastal locations around Britain suffered from such attacks as late as the early 19th century. However, the major change to Ravenglass seems both related to the changing coastline and the enthronement of James 1 of England (VI Scot) and thus the end of the Reivers – who had taken advantage of the lack of any true law and order within the debateable territories of England

Ravenglass Main Street.

STAGE 1

Holly House.

The Pennington.

and Scotland to wage continual warfare between themselves and everyone else that might have something worth acquiring. Having the same King, equalled a united authority to deal with the problem and Cumbria suddenly saw bastles, pele towers and castles suddenly relaxing their defences and becoming domestic farmhouses and grand mansions with wide windows and embellishment rather than battlements replacing dusty old Castles. Former top Reivers* were departing for foreign parts or becoming respectable and eliminating their own compatriots to ensure their own survival, with designs on

---

* Riever; or Border Reivers. Politically adept over-enthusiastic entrepreneurs; solidly believing in the free market (as long as this involved everyone else's market); not frightened to take a direct approach to commodity trading (stealing cattle) and social engineering (burning people alive) to gain market share. The savvy ones saw that the game was up with the Act of Union and became respectable gentlemen of commerce.

Ravenglass old petrol station.

some serious money-making out of the land, or to be precise what was underneath – coal and haematite, to mention but two.

Why are the cottages on the main street in Ravenglass so close to the river Mite and the convergence with the river Irt and Esk, which is a potentially perilous location for living?

There is an explanation for this near aquatic life and it appears to have been a mixture of commercial common sense, weighing the risk of being on the beach with being available to do immediate business. Added to this, nearby Muncaster Castle decided to tidy up its immediate environs with the end of border problems with Scotland and

Irish Sea in the distance.

STAGE 1

Who pulled the plug out?

The Green.

The yacht 'Acme' at rest: pride of the Ravenglass fleet.

Safe anchorage.

River Mite ford – mud and fast flowing water, use the footbridge!...

with it a wish to begin to make itself into a grand establishment. This meant that the locals, who had lived by the Castle for its safety, found themselves moved down the hill to the beach so as not to use up any valuable agricultural land. Take a look at the house dates in Ravenglass – they all seem to postdate 1603 when James succeeded to the English throne.

But the fact that these structures are actually built on the hard,

...which is close by, to the right. You can see it this side of the River Mite viaduct.

preventing ships from accessing the facility, indicates a change in usage and the pinch points at either end to help with livestock movement suggests a whole new phase in the port management. The stabilisation of the area, starting with the construction of the hard, continues with resulting cumulative quantities of silt depositing itself at Ravenglass from the river Mite as increased call upon the forest of Miterdale and Eskdale for the burgeoning coal and iron mining industry, further North at Whitehaven, continues apace. This deforestation begins a wholesale erosion of the Fells and a clogging up of navigable part of the Mite waterway. The river Esk seems to have become more important and the access, egress to shipping at Ravenglass moves naturally from south, north to east-west with cattle being moved across the upper part of the hard, rather than down the slope into the ships.

There is indication of massive sawn oak timbers beneath the buildings and street, suggesting that the street started life as a purpose-built hard for beaching vessels. The construction was to prevent erosion by the river Mite. The construction favoured craft specifically built to be beached; flat bottomed – perhaps grain carriers and barges.

Many historians suggest Ravenglass was chosen as a port because of the convergence of three rivers. This is not the case – the river Irt only turned towards Ravenglass in relatively recent times and the original course of the Esk likewise suggests that initially only the Mite provided a depth of water for large sea-going vessels in Ravenglass at the time of the Romans, with the Esk taking its place as the Mite choked. The arrival of the River Irt in Ravenglass appears to coincide with its demise as a port, suggesting that the two are linked; the channel into the port had changed making passage more difficult. Clearly with the iron ore close at hand in the Eskdale valley and coal mining well advanced around Whitehaven by the eighteenth century, putting the two together would have proved advantageous (as Whitehaven had found to its profit), but it was not to be and when iron ore was sent to Ravenglass it was to be in railway wagons for export, not for production on the spot. Otherwise Ravenglass would probably be a very different place today.

Eskdale had been involved in the iron industry from before the Romans and the main factor in respect of production was the well-managed coppicing for charcoal, so much so that records indicate the importation of ore by packhorse into the dale from Egremont because of the plentiful fuel supply. Charcoal production didn't affect the rivers because the trees were not felled and therefore there was no erosion;

the coal production did, through tree-felling for pit props for the mines; this in turn clogged the rivers, due to erosion deposits, so any proposal for boats to deliver coal from the mines in reasonable quantity to make it worthwhile considering setting up furnaces at Ravenglass would require considerable investment in harbour facilities outweighing the viability of a foundry. This is a somewhat simplified scenario, but it does match an erstwhile attempt to improve the navigation into Ravenglass with a series of navigation markers in the early part of the 19th century.

Watch for the Tide

Note. If the tide is in follow the signs from the village centre marked 'Bath House'.

If the Tide is In

The Bath House

These are grand ruins, un-touched, no repair work here; they are as they were. There is clear evidence of alterations to the building, most probably post Roman re-use.

The Bath House remains because it was a relatively small, well-built building that could be defended. A good strong set of walls, originally holding up a domed roof in parts, makes an excellent bastion against attack. The walker should note that some of the walls still have their original decoration, and in particular look at the east-facing wall. Take

The way forward.

The Bath House.

STAGE 1

Dappled way to the bathhouse.

The Roman Bath House.

a close look – it is not restored, it really is as was. This is a genuinely remarkable survival from another age; the care and attention of the construction and the deliberately defined colour change gives an intimate moment – for a brief moment the viewer feels as if the building is complete, not on the edge of a field.

With the world changing drastically for the locals after the end of Roman control meant coastal locations were profitable but dangerous places to be – the thick walls of the bath house were a better bet than a fort which was too big to defend.

The Roman idea of defence is to go out and attack the enemy, which is why Roman forts have four gates. If you are attacked at one you can go out and attack the attacker via the other three. But this calls for a disciplined, well-armed force with training and back up. This simply isn't available after the collapse because the link between the individual and the State has gone – no central government, represented in its basic form, that of a currency, means there are no bonds, no trust and no desire to conform to a central power that has deserted the individual to their fate. The Bath House is the last vestige of organisation and that, by its size, could have housed one or two extended families rather than a whole community. There is evidence of a wooden staircase in the building suggesting that the structure was converted, with up floors possibly suggesting a hierarchy of leaders that lived above the smell and noise of the common Hall, which probably lay on top of the filled-in baths themselves. The water supply from the extensive reservoir in the woods above would have been diverted, but the fact that there was running water would have been advantageous. Later references to this site suggest that in the 8th-9th century it was a 'palace'; considering it had stood by then for six hundred years or more and still had a water supply, in comparison with everything else it probably was!

The fields beyond, to the East, are part of the vicus, the civilian settlement around the fort, in this case because Ravenglass is a port; this is a much larger establishment than would otherwise be the case. The lure of trade with the rest of the Roman Empire would attract traders – export of timber, wool and iron would require administrators, tradesmen and slave labour. All would require services.

The Fort

Across the way from the Bath House. To the casual eye – just a field – but the ditches give the site away. The area closest to the gate is the eastern corner of the fort, lost with the construction of a Victorian greenhouse, which in turn is archaeology, although residents of Ravenglass can remember playing in its ruins. Reports of the tiled floor suggest that there had been re-use of material, possibly from the bath house, in its construction. Greenhouse aside, the site is tidy enough and the east and north facing ditches are plain enough.

The fort is a much sorrier site from the seaward side, cut through by the railway and eroded by the sea. The late Dr Timothy Potter and Prof. David Shotter excavated the eroding edge in 1976. A thorough excavation for its day, it was carried out with the knowledge that the elements would eventually catch up with the site, which they now have done with incredible fury. Cascades of pottery, tile and burnt timbers are a regular occurrence. Every request for emergency action to retrieve material in a formal way, in what context that can be discerned from the mess, has been denied. It's a world heritage site slowly melting away, with the official line that all that could be done was done in 1976; however they do not take into account that not all was recovered and the findings on the very last day of the dig, had time and

The approach to the Roman fort.

Red sandstone block from the fort – valuable pre cut stone; handy ballast.

Ravenglass Fort – more to it than meets the eye.

Severe erosion on the seaward side of the Fort.

circumstance allowed, would have changed the date of the fort forever. More on this anon.

Walkers can make their minds up about the condition of the fort. Go and see.

What happened to the fort is easy enough to explain. With the collapse of the Roman world in the West (the bit that is complicated) aside, the fort was pulled down for ballast for ships trading through

Summer flowers in the fort ditch.

STAGE 1

Southern end of fort site, which the sea will soon turn into an eroded embankment – railway is in cutting at this point, just over the gorse.

Ravenglass – excellent high quality, high value ballast and in nice regular shapes. From the destruction layers it went pretty quickly as there is little vegetation in the rubble field.

> *The collapse of the Roman Empire in the West is a slower process than readily understood, mainly brought about by the division of the Roman Empire into two halves, East and West, and the obvious division of power and internal strife. Add to this the devaluation of coinage to pay troops and taxes associated with internal conflict, climate change causing food shortages and epidemics, with a good dollop of self determination and emergent nationalism over tribalism.*

You were warned!

If the Tide is Out

After the walker has enjoyed the main street of Ravenglass, head through the big metal gates at the end of the street (which hold the tide back when things get a tad rough, as they are wont to do when the spring tides, fuelled by a so-westerly wind, meet a swollen set of rivers after a good downpour in the Fells), at the west end and down on to the beach to enjoy the view. Note the Eskmeals Range Sign. It is safe to walk here, but just note the details and do not be alarmed by the odd bang. To your right the river Irt imperceptibly spills across the mud towards Ravenglass; it doesn't really want to come this way and objects by spreading itself out into a series of barely connected pools no more than a knee deep in summer. The dunes hold the sea at bay, but less every year; the gates at the end of main street prevent flooding, but for how much longer the walker can surmise. Turn left along the old coast road, still a right of way heading towards Bootle, (so mind for the occasional 4x4). Cross the stream, which is from the sewage works and is on the same course as one of the drains from the vicus – some things never change – and head on to the headland. This gives an excellent vantage point over the whole scene. Go off down the steps and across one of the drains from the bath house and vicus, still working as it has for over two thousand years. Even the railway took this little water course into account and no doubt its present 'cover' is made of Roman fort material. Along the rough path the walker will then be confronted by a headland much destroyed by the sea. This is the western edge of Ravenglass fort. The walker will wish to know that this catastrophic mess is an English Heritage, grade one listed structure; also and more importantly a World Heritage Site. The walker will note black layers and areas of compressed stone in the cross section neatly cut by the waves – these are the remains of barrack room floors and destruction layers and rebuilding.

The walker is advised, should they desire to make their opinion known, to consider a formal complaint at the highest level. The author suggests the:

Minister of State
Dept of Culture Media & Sports
2-4 Cockspur Street
London
SW1Y 5DH

The body that tells English Heritage what to do.

There you are, you are getting involved in archaeology and it's only day one!

Continue walking along the beach until you reach a railway bridge. If you wish to have a short circular walk turn left under its arch, and left again at the top of the rise; the walker will soon be alongside the fort again and the bath house.

For those wanting to walk to Muncaster Castle, turn left under the bridge and right at the top of the rise. DO NOT TURN RIGHT – it is private property. Look for the blue Muncaster sign. The path takes you along the edge of the vicus; the path gives a brief glimpse down to the sea before arriving at a junction where the walker should turn left and on a steady climb travel through a small valley. A dam and pond are soon reached. This is a recent reconstruction of an earlier dam, which in turn was a replacement for an even earlier one. The present path would have been at least a metre under the original water level as it traverses the present reservoir. There is evidence of a weir and the present Decoy Pond (used to attract wildfowl) is the remains of the sump for the Bath House far below. This piece of Roman hydraulic engineering was still supplying water along lead pipes to water troughs in the fields below into what was the vicus until the 20th century when the lead was dug up. There is also evidence of excavation of ore in the area and some of attempts at iron working.

Continue along the main path through the gate and up the hill. To the left there is significant evidence of medieval agricultural works, but also of earlier enclosures and some structure bases. To the right is poor degraded land below the rise of Newton Knot. As the walker approaches a modern looking pagoda (the ticket office for the castle) the walker should look to the right. The land is much improved and the eye is drawn over to the tree line. This is the Intake, a natural break in the lie of the land that allows cattle to be funnelled into a safe area when the Reivers, or others, were on the prowl for easy pickings.

The ticket office offers entrance to the gardens of Muncaster Castle.

Muncaster Castle

The walker will be immediately struck by the wide variety of rhododendrons, camellias and azaleas. The gardens of Muncaster are a delight to the eye because they surprise at any time of year. But the Muncaster Castle is of another order – nothing is as it seems. The author, having excavated and lived within its walls, can honestly report that there really is nowhere else quite like it. A single visit is not enough; the more you delve the more you will find.

The Pennington family has lived at Muncaster for over eight hundred years. The site is much older. The location, protected from the blast of the sea (being hidden behind Newton Knott, overlooking the river Esk) provides a sentinel at a crossroads – the west-east up the river and the north-south crossing point of the same. It was this that intrigued the author enough to excavate Muncaster in an attempt to identify its origins.

It has always been suggested that Muncaster has Roman

foundations. The author cannot disagree, nor agree, as he never got deep enough beneath the structure to find out. At 12 metres below the ground, still in later construction rubble, he gave up. What he did find was an immense ditch, defensive in nature – now completely filled in – that prevented access to the castle along what is now the path from the Stable Yard to the clock tower side of the castle. This ditch provided the third side of a regular card-shaped feature, potentially a fort, the other two sides, very obvious by their prominence, overlooking the valley. By research the fourth side was identified under the meadow just beyond the formal lawns and garden gates on the west side of the castle.

It's the right shape for a fort, there's a good ditch, even clear evidence of a well-built road coming straight up from the river crossing towards it, but absolutely no evidence of who built it – no Roman pottery and whilst Roman coin is known from the grounds, no evidence from the excavation whatsoever of a fort itself. Frustrating in the extreme. But these things happen and hopefully when the castle can afford the funds further investigations will take place. There has been a successful investigation into the internal features by English Heritage, supported by local volunteers involved in community archaeology projects, which has considerably enhanced our understanding of the place.

The amount of change is graphically illustrated by the activity underneath the playground lawns across from the Stable Yard near the duck pond. Dug in the 1950s to supply water just in case the castle caught fire (the only other regular water supply capable of supplying enough in a hurry being the river), it was an area that had previously been a nine-hole golf course. And sometime before that there were the houses of servants and staff, all of which went down the hill when the castle was gentrified in the 17th century.

Take time to look at the curious folly features on the entrance walls to the Stable Yard. These fitments are examples of adornments that every castle in the 18th century just had to have. There are paintings showing the whole castle in this folly guise.

The woodland gardens contain rhododendrons, camellias and azaleas; spectacular and joyous. There is also a lost garden, with raised beds to allow a disabled member of the Pennington family in Victorian times to enjoy gardening. It is a rare discovery, forgotten and charming. See if you can find its remains. There are many hidden gems worthy of the walker's time.

The castle has a magnificent vista over lower Eskdale and the walker should note that the view, only two hundred years ago, would have been very different than today. The tidal flow would engulf much that is now meadow and pastureland. The building of a causeway and bridge over the Esk in the early part of the nineteenth century began a process of silting up of the lower Esk – a process that was duly completed by the building of the railway viaduct for the Barrow-in-Furness to Whitehaven line. This process was exacerbated as a result of intense deforestation in Eskdale, while coppicing for charcoal production had been carried out for centuries the intensity of the production had taken on a new phase, with charcoal being produced for the Broughton blast furnace complex to the south, which sucked in immense quantities of material to keep its furnace fed. Ultimately it drained the landscape to such an extent that it became unviable and the process and staff moved to Scotland. The damage had been done – erosion caused by grubbing out of coppicing after the Broughton furnace collapse. An increase in more intense mining techniques and the first modern attempts to control the flow of the Esk led to a clogging up along the eastern side of the causeway and the viaduct finished the job. Although the sea and the river do still make their presence known at spring high tides, the walker lucky enough to be at Muncaster on such dates can witness a glimpse of what lower Eskdale looked like not that long ago as the causeway submerges for an hour or so and the verdant green pasture turns to silver.

This silver thread leads the walker back to a time when sailing craft made the journey to Roman kilns to load with pottery and tiles – to meet with smaller craft loaded with iron and wool. Passing by the island at Lower Eskholme you will witness where the tax office probably stood, in an exposed location hardly above the tide, but worth the discomfort for the greedy tax collector.

If the walker could stand on the roof of the castle, which the author has done, it is possible to see right up Eskdale towards Hardknott.

Firstly this is a magnificent view – "The Gateway to Paradise" – and should be considered as one of the finest views in Britain. The view to the actual fort is a disputed one, with suggestion of an intermediate signalling post in Eskdale. The author, from experience of digging the site, leans toward Professor David Shotter, Lancaster University's opinion that Muncaster was at least a signalling station and considers the possibility of a series of such stations to be a credible one – be it as a solitary station or attached to a fort – is still to be settled by further work.

Secondly and what is not in dispute is the fact that Muncaster sits on a crossroads. The river running east to west and a road running north to south (or vice versa) makes it an important spot; it has no responsibility for what happens on the coast, it is sheltered from the Cumbrian 60mph 'breeze' and sits close to a fordable point of the river.

Archaeological research (which is in its early stages) on the Roman road to the south of the river Esk suggests that the present route over Corney Fell may have partially incorporated at least one inland route, with another more coastal route quite easily traceable between Bootle and Millom. As for forts and other establishments, research has been patchy. Give us archaeologists time and a bit of cash and we will get there!

The author will never forget witnessing one of his senior archaeologists, a lady of mature years, rock climbing out of the trench rather than using the ladder. It was a very deep excavation, seventeen feet below the cellar floors! Patrick Gordon Duff Pennington, the patriarch of the castle, would always introduce the author as, "This is Clifford, he's undermining the Castle". The author considers this an exaggeration but would concede that it was a big hole and the bottom of the original ditch was never reached, but the ditch did provide a north-east facing edge to a fort platform within the recognised dimensions of a Roman fort, giving perhaps a glimpse of Roman occupation of the site, but not enough and no pottery at all!

Thirdly, it is the presence, the imposition on the landscape that is often overlooked; by being at the castle you do not view it because you are there. The viewer from the south sees a very powerful establishment imposing a strong presence, a statement that passage is with its permission. Up close the castle has an amiable personae, it is no barrier at all, not in its present form; it has a folly quality that can be best described as homely.

But the walker should consider there is some underlying echo of place, of slumbering power beneath the present charm; that whilst the present is an architectural canvas, much reworked with bits flaking off, the foundations know differently.

More importantly this house (for that is what it really is), lived in, loved, and the scene of continuing family life, beats at a different pace. The castle is a family – not just the Pennington's but the staff who keep it operational. The conference facilities, the wedding receptions and marriages, and the Tom Foolery all keep the place busy, vibrant, a tad crazy, a smidgen quirky and not without the odd bizarre twist. But that's what makes it very real, very personable and much loved. A castle with a heart, a past and a future.

Thomas Skelton, claimed by some to be the last "Fool" or jester in

England, was in residence at the Castle as estate bailiff, until 1659. He came in rather useful for the author in his archaeological investigation. In the gardens close to the Castle is a tree, Tom Fool's tree, reputed to be where Tom would send travellers to their doom if he didn't like them by sending them across the river Esk into the quicksands; lovely chap, great sense of humour, very hospitable. The reality is rather different. Thomas, in his role as bailiff, would be responsible for collecting tolls and the control of the road north to south which at the time was undoubtedly right past the door of the castle. The present tree does not date back to the sixteenth century, but the location for Thomas collecting the toll for passing the Castle would have to be paid thereabout. No toll payment and a soaking was assured, and a legend of an evil reputation born. But, more importantly, the collection of a toll equalled a road and a road there was, straight down the hill from the tree – reasonably intact and deliberately hidden by trees planted in the late 18th century when the new formal drive was constructed. This earlier road had all the hallmarks of a well-constructed Roman road. Alas, all is now destroyed. The author's archaeological excavation was one large trench; a storm hit western Cumbria in 2003 and devastated the forestry close to the castle and the trench became one of many casualties as great and beautiful trees were ripped from the ground. The road was all but destroyed. It looked like the Battle of the Somme; too dangerous with the fallen trees to work in the area and with the need for the trees to be removed and thus all hope of recovering the site was lost. These things happen, but had it not been for Tom Fool and his tree the Roman road would probably never have been seen at all. Now at least it is known and the way down to the river is identified.

The walker may ask what next? Time will tell that and funding.

It comes as no surprise that Muncaster is haunted as the author knows only too well.

This was no dark night, with trees thrashing in the gentle Cumbrian breeze, with owl screeching as portents of the coming of the dead experience (there is no shortage of the latter, that is owls, as the world-renowned World Owl Trust is based in the gardens! Do give them a visit and support their work). The dead, the author is reliably informed by a member of the Pennington family, "tend to divide into two categories – the indoor ghosts and the outdoor ghosts, but they do, from time to time pop in, or out to enjoy a bit of a change," and the author has no doubt that they do. We all need a change of scene from time to time and the dead do have the advantage of not paying the entrance fee!

This was a daylight experience with no physical cause and no immediate rational explanation; but the haunting of the author introduced him to the work of Dr Jason Braithwaite, an acknowledged expert on Brain Behavioural Science at Birmingham University and his long-term research at Muncaster into the magnetic variances associated with such haunting experiences. The author, like Dr Braithwaite, is a sceptic in respect of the haunting experience, being an occurrence of the dead visiting the living, but inexplicable sounds and the sensation of presence is perceptibly fear-making in anyone, especially in broad daylight, when it is the sound of an axe chopping wood by the author's left ear.

Dr Braithwaite's experiments conducted in the trenches beneath the castle had interesting results; those interested in such matters should consult Dr Braithwaite.

Take the tour of the house and enjoy the gardens – this is why the author strongly suggests that the first day of the walk never takes you out of the parish. Take the time and consider the perspective. Could there have been a Roman signal station here, or a fort? Where was the crossing point of the Esk? Was there a series of wharves?

After enjoying the castle and gardens, which should take a good three or four hours at the very least, retrace your steps. When you reach the junction on Walls Drive, bear right. On the walker's left is the fort and, on the right, a short distance away, is the bath house. The path will then take you back into Ravenglass for a good meal and several pints, offering time to reflect on the sheer majesty of a tiny bit of West Cumbria hidden away from the world.

There is much to see and do, but take time to sit on the benches on the village green and enjoy the marvel of a Ravenglass sunset.

Let the Train Take the Strain
A Fast Trip to Hardknott

Those walkers on a limited timescale should consider the Ravenglass & Eskdale railway as an option to get them to Dalegarth, Boot, quickly. The railway operates virtually throughout the year, but the service understandably is restricted in the winter. To thoroughly enjoy a relaxing day in Eskdale and Hardknott catch the first train of the day to Dalegarth, Boot. This will normally be a diesel service, but check the timetable for the first steam train. The locomotive fleet is nearly equally balanced between steam and diesel; steam predominates, but the Ravenglass & Eskdale has always been at the forefront of traction design and usage, and the *Douglas Ferreira,* the new Society-owned diesel is a fine example of that tradition. Whilst people will always talk of the romance of steam, the reality of a wild wet West Cumbrian afternoon in October with very limited protection on the footplate of the steam engines, other than a thick mackintosh, makes romance melt away; the delights of a heated cab and a proper comfortable seat wins every time.

The Ravenglass & Eskdale Railway has a truly fascinating history; do take the opportunity to enjoy a trip, travelling in an open coach hauled by a steam engine is virtually unique in the UK and the views are simply spectacular. There is an excellent railway museum at Ravenglass that uses the ex-Furness railway waiting room. The efforts of the curator and engine driver Peter Van Zeller and volunteers are to be commended. The restored main line signal box and its garden is likewise a tribute to the efforts of individuals, which complements the village.

The journey is an exhilarating one and the author will not give the game away. The walker should travel in an open coach, or at the very least a semi-open (offering some protection from the elements) to get the real feel of the experience and the scenery flying by. Mind out for the smuts and don't rub your eye if you get one. The author was a guard and booking clerk on the railway for many years. He knows the line well.

The railway is partially constructed on the route of an ancient pack horse route into Eskdale; evidence of this is apparent from time to time along the way between Miteside Loop and Horsefalls, where the track heads down to an old ford, now lost by works to stop flooding of the Mite.

The train will deposit you at Dalegarth, Boot, station and you are in the heart of the dale with a considerable number of options to hand. But, if tight for time, turn left out of the station, minding the traffic (which can be considerable) on this minor byway and head for the crossroads by the Brook House Inn.

From here the walker should refer to Day Two as to what to do next.

The railway has a full-time staff aided by volunteers; it's very likely the guard of your train is one. Please support their efforts by considering membership of the Ravenglass & Eskdale Preservation Society. Your subscription and assistance will be put to good use; you never know you may want to volunteer. Further details at the end of this guide.

Stage Two

Walking From Ravenglass to Boot

This is a long day and to gain the full benefit a start just after seven in the morning is a must. The walking conditions are variable, but overall good. Be aware of unfenced drops and open water. Supervision of children is required throughout this walk.

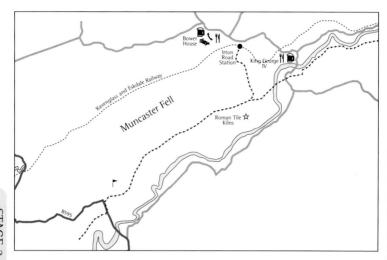

STAGE 2

If the tide is in, use the route to Muncaster Castle

As per tradition, feel free to have a boot-dipping ritual on the beach. Then, head south along the clearly marked (on the ordnance map) Cumbria Coastal Way, pass the fort and do not go under the railway bridge – simply go up and over the Swine Ghyll back on to the beach saving wet feet. The old track to Brighouse Farm and the coast road is pretty clear. The gateway to the site of the old farm still stands, enclosing a small field cut through by the railway. Contrary to local popular myth, Brighouse farm was not destroyed to build the railway, it survived that interruption; it seems to have succumbed to the possibility of erosion from the estuary, which in fact never came. The new farm sits on private property on the other side of the railway embankment. Keep close to the fence on the estuary side of the line as you will have to cross a very deep ditch with little or nothing more than collapsed masonry to support you. The way can be a tad soggy underfoot, but it is not impassable; with care this is an enjoyable route. The embankment and viaduct over the river Esk comes into view, and what an impressive structure it is. The beach road parallels the viaduct and fords the Esk; do not attempt this, nor attempt to cross the viaduct, as both can kill. The path passes under the railway into the reed beds which provide a maze-like journey, again somewhat damp on occasions but an enjoyable experience and the views open up every now and again, yielding a marvellous panorama of lower Eskdale. Waberthwaite church sits across the Esk on a site associated with the Roman crossing point. There is still, technically, a crossing point here, but a boat would be required to do it. The walker is now on the well-constructed Victorian 'River Drive' of Muncaster Castle. This is good walk, high above the river, with magnificent views. There is a sense of other worldliness. Time plays tricks here. The presence of the past is close. The Drive heads up towards the castle; if not going to the castle turn right through the bushes and down on to the pastures below the Castle.

If you are going to the castle via this route you are duly bound to purchase a ticket upon reaching it. The General Office, located in the Coach House, will oblige. The only public footpath across this part of the estate is via Newton Knott to Muncaster Church.

The bushes crowd in on the walker, the old estate wall is reached and suddenly the way is clear and the walker can enjoy the experience of being out in the open in good parkland, provided it's not raining! A short distance across the river plain, with good views up towards the bulk of the Castle, the A595 is now reached where care should be taken. Turn left and walk up the road and then turn right at the bottom of Muncaster Hill. The way is well marked. The route is through the golf course (keep to the path and watch out for the golf balls); apart from some damp patches before the golf course, this is very enjoyable walking.

Muncaster Head: slag from 17th century bloomery.

It's amazing what you learn from having a couple of pints in the pub (it's the natural environment for archaeologists), and such research should not be overlooked. The author has oft taught his students the worth of such study.

Somewhere in this stretch are the remains of a grand Roman building, the floors of which were seen in the 1960s and quietly covered up again. There is no academic record of this work, but the source of the information is sound. One day the author will do his best to verify the location – but there is much else to do in the meantime!

STAGE 2

The route runs at the base of Muncaster fell and at SD131986 the Park House Tile Kiln site is reached. Not obvious when you arrive at the site, even the sign is now a monument in its own right, but in the scrub behind, to the left of the path and in the fields around there are key signs of Roman pottery workings. There is even an earlier route of the path, lost in the woods, the section being abandoned because the steamroller couldn't make it through. Some of the pottery kilns were used as coal bins whilst the roller was in the area. The author has researched the area over many years and one finding suggests that most of the pottery from this early second century site left by boat, there being clear remains of a small harbour facility (this feature is not on public land).

The walker should pause as the scenery is worth more than a mere glance; the old road is hidden in the rhododendrons. The fell side at this point still holds secrets about the size of the pottery site – Mary Fair, the archaeologist responsible for putting West Cumbria on the archaeology map in the 1920s, excavated the site and discovered an intact kiln with its load of pottery still intact. What caused it to be left in such a state is open to debate. The clay supply seems not to have been worked out. The author suspects that by the second century AD when the kilns went cold for the last time, they being no longer required because the Romans were using slate rather than making tiles for the roofs of building (indicating the inter-relationship with the environment and the people within it, because of the skills needed to work the material) and the pottery produced was being supplanted by cheap imports, or possibly a shortage of timber for burning.

The author knows of other whole firings that have been found and considers the possibility that the potter, having exploited the soil, is paying back to the Gods that which he has taken away, by leaving a range of the goods he has made in payment or 'tribute' for same. This is the author's idea and he's sticking to it!

The use of waterborne transport should be of no great surprise as it is the easiest way of moving goods about; all the walker has to do is imagine the water back and Eskdale is then a very different place than it is today. This does open up the puzzling question of the road at the kiln. The author does not rule out the probability of a local road system; the practicalities of life cannot wholly rely on the waterway. The kilns would require timber for the firings and a system of collection. Carts were obviously being used by the works to keep the way level; there is evidence of the road system from near the golf course to just before Muncaster Head farm, where this local system bears away towards a significant area of iron production dating back to the Romans. This suggests a local road. Not a military highway.

The clay workings for the tile kilns can be clearly seen in fields close to the path as the walker heads on towards Muncaster Head farm. The way is delightful; over a small bluff and down to the farm where time and nature has smoothed out the past industry.

The path trundles over a pleasant wooded rise and a junction of paths will hove into view. The junction is significant; there is the path the walker is on from the Esk estuary via the kilns, the path coming down from Muncaster Fell; the path that takes you to Irton and another to Eskdale Green, plus the path over to Sword House and yet another that that trundles back along the Esk to a fording point (not to be recommended) over it heading then across the fells towards Corney. Thus the farm, Muncaster Head, although a relatively modern building, sits on a very significant coming together of the ways.

A Suggested Excursion

There is nothing better than a diversion to create a little extra adventure and turning left just before the farm house at Muncaster Head is a very good way of starting such an enterprise.

The way is very clearly marked as a proper wide farm track, initially at the edge of the present farm's activities, so mind out for cattle and tractors. The way is hard under foot, if a little claggy if the cows are about. The track does narrow, but its character is purposeful and was a regular through route until property boundaries changed and it was reduced to a footpath. This stroll is an easy one, with the destination at the Bower House Inn – truly a magnificent Inn of considerable age and character which, as the author knows very well, offers an excellent pint.

Along the way the walker should enjoy the scene but use eagle eyes, for there is much to deduce from the landscape.

This is distinctively different territory from the river. Climbing up from one valley, over to another – from Eskdale into Miterdale, on the stub end of the Fell, the very nature of place takes on that transition from one distinct dale landscape to another – a state of transition is truly apparent. The walker is bordering marginal land, not short of nutrients on the lower slopes, but heavily waterlogged. Immediately through the gate adjacent to the farm there is a junction of paths, one coming down from the Fell, another crossing the field with a footpath towards Eskdale Green station, via a stretch of beck. There is more to these crossroads than mere paths crossing – there are remains of a settlement hereabouts, which the Eskdale Historical Society has done much good work on.

To the left is gorse acting as a skirt to the bulk of the Fell; hidden within its sharp edges are bloomery sites dating back to the Romans, to the right once the track levels out; fields with closely cropped grass and in the distance are indications of Bronze Age works, including a burial cairn. Continual activity along this important north-south route from one dale to the next cannot be overlooked and the fact bloomery sites have been discovered here suggests that the proximity of the route, to allow for easy charcoal delivery and finished product transportation, is a key feature. Today, all the walker sees is a pleasant rural way. The signs of the past are there, it's just a case of finding them.

The track takes on a layer of tarmac and a switch back approach to keeping a direct line.

Irton Road station is soon reached – a glorious piece of industrial history, still doing the job just as it was in 1875 when it was built. The station was a significant contributory factor in the fact that many of the houses in Eskdale Green owe their existence to the ease in which modern building materials could be delivered direct to the dale by rail. It also acted as a gateway to the middle classes to live away from the smoke of Barrow and Whitehaven by commuting via the Ravenglass & Eskdale and its transhipment point with the Furness Railway at Ravenglass. The bridge over the station indicates the fact the railway was originally 3-foot gauge; the station building dates from those long gone days, but it still is very busy and is a centre for the railway to

The last of the flat lands.

STAGE 2

receive ballast deliveries and where the railway cuts and stores firewood which provides an additional income.

The author has spent many pleasant days as Stationmaster at Irton Road. On busy days, as two trains pass each other in opposite directions, there can be frenetic activity for five minutes and then peace for another thirty. It's not a bad way to spend the day – the odd ticket sale, perhaps a chat with the permanent way train crew that has scuttled into the siding; time for a chat and wait for the hot pasties to arrive from Dalegarth café, delivered by the guard from the next Ravenglass-bound train. A quick curse under the breath because the Dalegarth bound is late again and the driver is, as ever, in a world of his own – the guard raising his hands in sublimation just waiting for the end of his shift. There was once a plan to build a line from Irton Road to the Bower House. There was even a first sod cutting ceremony, but sadly it came to nothing.

A happy, unique and timeless place, where the past and present combine. Trains pass and may they continue to do so for many years to come.

Past the station road end and the walker then meets the main road through the dale. At the road junction turn left, but beware the road as it is narrow and a country lane but busier than you might think!

The old Methodist chapel on the right is now a house and a little further along the rather stern profile of the cottages which contained the police house swing into view. Just before the cottages is the turning for Miterdale – another adventure for another day. Keep straight on, but beware the corner because it's blind. Past the garage and a quick pace away, over the river Mite, you will find the Bower House; a gem of an Inn. A truly excellent spot to contemplate the journey so far over several pints and a fine meal, or an enjoyable overnight stay in the most hospitable of atmospheres.

The author is convinced that there is a mill associated with this inn as virtually every other flow of water in the dale has at one time been utilised to turn a wheel. As there is no shortage of supply and gravity is providing a helping hand, the gentle beck that flows through the garden must once have been a useful agent of some process or other. Perhaps the author may one day excavate; it is of course part of an Inn and therefore of particular interest – what else does an archaeologist do at the end of the day?

The walker will soon understand the magic of the place, be it winter, by the fire, or summer in the garden with the sound of a cricket match close by – Cumbria at its finest. And the author will not spoil the discovery by writing more.

You dwell a while longer than expected.

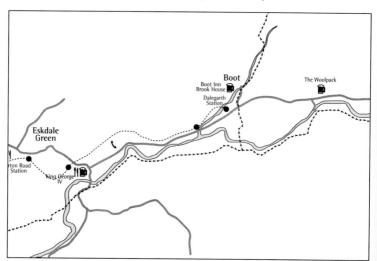

Keep straight on at the farm and the walker will notice a feature to the right – a slight mound in a field and closer a dry mill leet. This leet fed a waterwheel providing blowers and hammers to a forge. Fortunately, although nothing remains above ground, the site has been excavated and the site can be accurately dated to 1636. The site is important in understanding Eskdale, sited where it is for the water supply, but more importantly because of the amount of coppice wood available to keep such a massive investment commercially viable. Having such a facility in operation day and night would require a dedicated workforce – specialists in excavating ore, ironworkers, general hands, coppice workers and charcoal workers all needed feeding and housing. There is clear evidence that many farmers and smallholders in the dale also worked the mines and worked iron as and when they required, the skill passed down from one generation to the next.

Over the bridge and on to the Eskdale to Ulpha road where the walker should turn left, on to the open river plain with the field walls highlighting previous courses of the river Esk. The walker should turn right before the 'modern' Forge Bridge on to a well worn track, which keeps to the south bank of the river. However, some refreshment at the George IV should not be missed, especially as this means crossing the ancient river bed to its other bank, which gives clear indication of how things have changed. The George IV sits on a small peninsula of rock and takes full advantage of its foundation. Early photographs reveal that there were additional foundations that were tacked on to the rock; these seem to be far too grand in origin to be stables, which is how they ended their days before being demolished. However, the photo provided a clue for the author and after much research in the beer cellar (probably the best archaeological research the author has ever undertaken) samples of mortar indicated the building at least dates back to the 15th century. The cellar system is built into the rock and has little to do with the later building above. The floors were not lifted, for practical reasons, but there may be more to be found below. Time will tell.

Fully refreshed, the walker should retrace his/her steps over Forge Bridge and turn left on to the good path towards Milkingsteads. This is glorious walking; the river has been tamed for much of this stage and beyond Milkingsteads a suspension bridge brings a path in from Fisherground. The author has a suspicion that Fisherground is named after fish ponds; as a guard on the La'al Ratty he would often be sat in the loop (trains pass at Fisherground) and the outline of two long shallow enclosures are quite apparent in the adjacent fields below. It is worth walking out on to the middle of the bridge and enjoying the river, especially on a hot day. Such pleasant moments past and with the way ahead clear, the sound of the water refreshes the very soul. The path passes through a line of river-side trees, then on to an open field with the wall acting as the direction of the path. The walker should stop and look to the left, up to the fell side. A curious feature should meet the eye – a line from the top of the fell, falling straight towards the tree line at Fisherground. This is no natural feature, but an early incline from mines high on the fell. These workings predate the construction of the railway and are evidence of the size and effort of the exploitation of the dales riches over centuries.

Through the abandoned farm, a sea of stinging nettles and decay, nature reigns in decay. The path is very close to the river here and a slab of Mother Eskdale makes a very enjoyable paddling area for the feet. From here the path has recently been renewed and delivers the walker through woodland to the junction of paths before Stanley Ghyll.

The path was recently renewed, originally at river level with consequent problems when in spate. It did, however, reveal a very curious anomaly, that of an apparent wharf edge – a curious wall with rubble fill on its landward side, well constructed with remains of a watercourse coming up to its edge. The old riverside path actually climbed out of the river over it. This anomaly was combined with another significant man-made feature on the Birkby road on the opposite side of Eskdale, making the author consider the hypothesis of

Just stand back and take it all in.

waterborne transport in Eskdale at least as far as Milkingsteads and probably as far Stanley Gyhll. This was incredible to consider against the scene today, but the river was very different then and the craft would have been punts – still more efficient than wagons and pack horses. The feature was, for the most part, destroyed in the rebuilding. Fortunately a record was taken before the renewals were undertaken.

The walk through the woods towards Stanley Ghyll will, at one point, bring the walker down to the edge of a large swampy pond. The author considers this to be a significant industrial feature related to the nearby Hall.

The Ghyll is worth a detour – a narrow ravine with a spectacular waterfall. The path to the pools below it is good, but care should be taken the further up the walker goes. There is a path that allows you to exit the Ghyll at the top, and what a dramatic change in scenery the walker gets upon doing so!

Nature has a way of healing its scars. Nearby Dalegarth Hall is a charming farm house and barn, full of architectural bits of the earlier halls. It is, in reality, the heart of a major iron manufacturing base, owned by the Stanley family. The present house is the remains of a much larger residence, afforded by the fact the house stood at the centre of a constant pyroclastic display as thirty or more bloomeries were operated day and night creating the family wealth. The slag heaps from this activity can be found to the north west of the site, near the car park for Trough House Bridge.

Bloomeries

Bloomeries are clay-built chimneys, incorporating (on occasion) stone and earth, up to about 1.5m high. Near the bottom of the chimney, piercing through the side wall of the chimney is a single or series of clay pipes or tuyères; these are to force air into the furnace by means of hand-operated bellows. At the very bottom of the chimney there is an opening, normally roughly plugged whilst the process of iron production takes place, which can be released to allow for the removal of the bloom of iron.

The fuel for the production of the iron is charcoal. Much of Eskdale was put aside to coppice production to produce a near pure carbon fuel, ideal for the process. The iron ore (haematite readily available in Eskdale) is crushed down and warmed through to extract any moisture.

The bloomery is charged with charcoal, much as we would today with a barbecue, and oxygen is forced into it. The ore is then introduced and more charcoal is added, whereupon the charcoal releases carbon monoxide reducing the iron oxides in the ore to metallic iron. This process does not melt the ore, the bloomery operating at a temperature that is lower than the melting temperature of the ore. The skill of the ironmaster is to get the temperature and amount of charcoal to ore in relative balance.

The iron particles fall to the bottom of the bloomery and become welded into a bloom. Along with the particles of iron, the impurities in the ore also end up at the bottom, so some ends up in the bloom. This means it has to be reheated and beaten with a hammer to drive the molten slag out of it. Wrought iron is the result.

The clay chimneys don't survive the perils of time, but the slag, charcoal and iron fortunately do!

Having enjoyed the waterfall, the opportunity to get the boots wet and possibly more is provided by the stepping stones across the Esk at St Catherine's church.

If the river is too high do not despair, for the path on the East side of the river continues on and beneath the close cropped turf and bracken are the remains of charcoal burning platforms and bloomery sites. Such effort and energy of another age is lost in the gentle slopes beneath the wall-like fell edge.

The river and the fell decide to join forces and squeeze the path to a near pinch point. The walker should turn left when the path enters a small dark glade, to cross the river by 'The Girders'. The path to the bridge is not clear from the upper path and the descent to it is complicated at the last minute by a small stream. Be careful how you tread. The walker will be aware of the remains of industry; the bridge itself and the high riverside walls supporting a relatively slender strand of usable space for wagons to go into, or arrive out of the mines, for this is the site of Ghyll Foss mine which burrowed its way under the ever imposing Birker Fell above. The bridge brought the railway to the mine around 1881, but the mine, or at least the retaining riverside wall, pre-dates this date. There also seems to be a change of gauge for on the mine side of the bridge there is a spur to a spoil heap that suggests a gauge of 0.45metres. On the Boot side the gauge is 0.914metres, which was the gauge of the Ravenglass & Eskdale Railway at the time of its construction.

The walker can enjoy the Girder Bridge with a substantial and safe walkway on top of it. When the railway was cut back to what later became Dalegarth station, the original top of the bridge rotted away leaving just two girders over the rather nasty drop.

"The Girders" were always a challenge in their 'naked' form; the author braved them on his hands and knees, an inch by inch progression which appeared cowardly as a local lad passed him on the opposite girder merrily whistling a happy tune as he cycled across!

Having crossed, the remains of the railway become clear; the path will take you back towards St Catherine's church, which is certainly worth a second look, and then winds its way to the crossroads and the Brook House Inn. The walker has arrived in Boot.

Boot is a hamlet, but it prides itself in having two pubs, a railway station (Dalegarth), a watermill, art gallery, shop/post office, guest house and some very superior self-catering cottages.

For a moment in history Boot was a veritable Klondike. With the coming of the railway to export iron ore in 1875 the mines expanded production and the workforce likewise increased. Above Boot the red stains of the inclines built to drop the ore in wagons down the fell-side are now becoming eroded by time and slowly but surely being covered by grass and bracken. The remains of Nab Ghyll mines are fading away, but through the efforts of the Ravenglass & Eskdale Railway and its associated Preservation Society, the old terminus of the Railway at Boot – abandoned in the 1920s for the less steeply graded line to its terminus and more easily accessed site on the 'main' road at Dalegarth – has been kept to enjoy. The basic infrastructure of the station and the route is in good order. It's well worth an adventure. The inclines down from the mines, which meet this old railway at right angles, are extremely steep and eroded; please remember what comes down does not go up so please protect this site by limiting your investigations.

The present watermill, dating from Elizabeth the First's reign, with over five hundred years of service to the community, is now owned by the Eskdale Mill and Heritage Trust. Please do make a visit and a donation; you are supporting a wonderful piece of industrial archaeology that still works. To get to the Mill, the walker must pass over the packhorse bridge, dating from the 16th century. The site of the Mill is because of the water source, the Whillan Beck, which takes a fall here and the Mill takes advantage of this. It is not the only Mill to do so; there is one extant Mill on private property about a mile further up the beck and remains of much earlier ones nearby. The author suggests the walker should investigate where access is permitted, but don't fall in!

The bridge is quite wide for a pack horse bridge. This is not solely for the purpose of accessing the Mill, for the walker will note that the path continues past the Mill, through a gate and on to the fell. To the left is the railway and inclines, and straight on is the 'old corpse' road from Wasdale – known as such because of the need to bury the dead in St Catherine's church ground rather than Wasdale. The bodies were brought across here.

The route over the moor pre-dates Christianity; the way is as early as the first of humankind walking the forested uplands and deciding to settle near sources of water, waiting for the deer and boar to come to drink. Burnmoor is littered with the past, including stone circles and cairns. The early deforestation of the upland led to erosion (and much of the woodland food source vanishing), land being turned over to burial of the dead, the lower slopes being too steep. The silts in the valley were capable of sustaining crops, leading humankind to move down into the valley bottoms. There is some evidence that the early traversing of the valley required more than just tree felling, but also some formal administration of boundaries. The 'old corpse' road is distinctly well marked – it's just a case of knowing what to look for. Take a look at the base of the stone wall on the left hand side as you walk from The Brook House, towards Fell Foot Gallery. Firstly they are very thick from clearing stones from the fields, and secondly look closer at the base of the left-hand wall and compare it with the right. There is very good reason to consider the base stones of the wall on the left to pre-date the wall on the right and the actual present wall above it.

There is evidence that this small community is overlooked by a playing card shaped enclosure with four regular entrances, strategically preventing passage without observation on to the moor.

Fell Foot Gallery is a joy of a place. There are some superb works of art and it is typical of Cumbria that such jewels are hard to find, but worth the effort.

The author suggests that Boot and its environs should be the end of the second day. Those wishing to be as close to Hardknott Pass as possible should consider the Woolpack Inn and Eskdale YHA for the night; the difference for those wishing to stop in Boot is no more than an hour at the most, but that should be a consideration regarding the time the walker needs to be at the bottom of Hardknott in the morning. An early start is a must. There are numerous walks around Boot and at least three routes from Boot to the Woolpack Inn. See day three for one route. Remember time is of the essence for crossing the passes.

Eskdale is blessed with a very active historical society; it is very good to see much good work being done to bring the dale to life. In particular the society has been very active in bringing the work of the archaeologist Mary Fair to a wider audience. This enquiring mind (which is something all archaeologists need) recorded an immense amount of information regarding Eskdale. Most importantly she looked at the landscape in the whole; the nature, the people, she was part of what she saw and she brought her environment to life. She saw more than most; photographed, recorded and excavated. Her work was reported via the Cumberland & Westmorland Antiquarian & Archaeological Society, but through the efforts of Eskdale Historical Society much of her work is now available to a much wider audience.

If you want to know more use the internet:
http://www.edlhs.org.uk/maryfair.htm   or when in the dale ask around. Somebody will know somebody who is involved.

STAGE 2

Excursion

The walker may consider spending a whole day in and around Boot. There are numerous walks and opportunities for archaeological investigation.

Take a trip on the train, from Dalegarth, Boot, down to Eskdale Green, with a walk back to Boot over the fells to see more remains of mines and peat houses – the stores for the peat cuttings which have created some of the tarns on the fell tops. There is a great deal to see here; an overlay of history that intrigues.

A tramp over the corpse road to Wasdale is an enjoyable day, provided the weather is with the walker, and with ample time to look more closely at the stone circle and the numerous cairns. Burnmoor has many secrets and it gives them up very rarely; the walker is just as likely to see something that archaeologists and historians have not. If the walker considers something to be of archaeological interest in this open location and wishes to bring it to the attention of archaeologists, take plenty of compass readings to allow us to find the spot again. This patch across the Burnmoor is the responsibility of the National Trust and the LDNP.

The walker might just want to go swimming in the pools at St Catherine's, or watch the locals jumping off Trough House bridge (near Stanley Ghyll) into the deep waters below. Buy a work of art (which can be sent home and will be waiting for you on your return), enjoy a beer, feel the mill wheel rumble the ground and write a postcard home. As they say, 'chill'. It's very easy to do in Boot!

The author recalls a Christmas Eve many years ago with the then landlord of the Burnmoor Inn, as it was called in those days, playing his accordion; the singing of carols, glinting sparkles of flame in the glasses and spicy mulled wine – all protection from the bible black darkness and the brooding fells outside. Boot was a very small solitary light on a dark winter's night, but it burnt all the brighter for it.

How many generations had sat in that warm glow out of the winter blasts? Hunters, miners, farmers, all as one, sheltered for a moment from the harsh reality of making the dale live and work and thrive. It was all part of the cycle so well illuminated by the fire; of ancient stone and man burdened and put to the sweat of toil but unbowed and ready to take on the morning with no less fortitude than the day before.

I looked into the night and perhaps I saw in that Christmas moment the wayfarer's gentle passing. We all pass through Boot and travel on but never forget the coming.

Cumbrian colours, near Eskdale.

STAGE 2

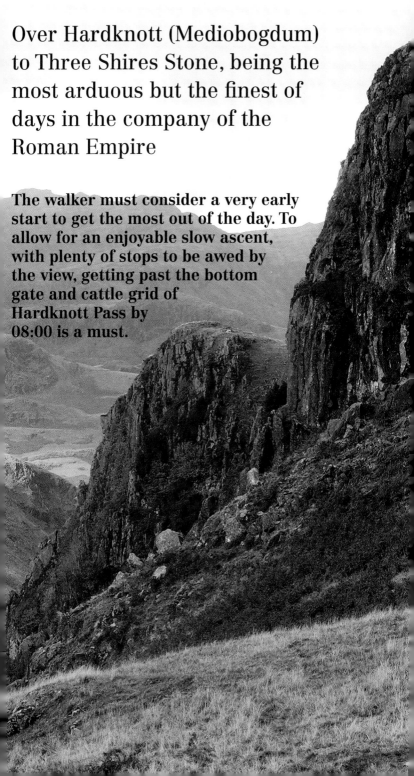

Stage Three

Over Hardknott (Mediobogdum) to Three Shires Stone, being the most arduous but the finest of days in the company of the Roman Empire

The walker must consider a very early start to get the most out of the day. To allow for an enjoyable slow ascent, with plenty of stops to be awed by the view, getting past the bottom gate and cattle grid of Hardknott Pass by 08:00 is a must.

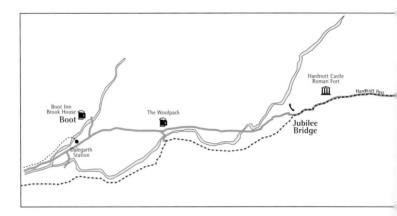

From the crossroads by the Brook House Inn, the walker should head towards St Catherine's Church and retrace his/her steps over the Girders Bridge. Turn left towards the deliberately destroyed entrance to the mines and follow along the edge of the river. Mind the edge. Just before the wall blocking further forward passage, the path zig-zags its way up to the lane. Turn left, through the gate and into relatively open, neatly cropped land (the Herdwicks do very good impressions of lawnmowers); this surreptitiously covers yet another piece of industrial heritage under its mantle. The fields here are the sites of charcoal burning activity, essential in the production of iron. The sweet smell of fresh air of today compares favourably with four hundred years ago

Bit steep!

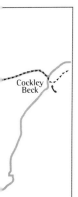

Cockley Beck

when it would have been a half hour of walking through a throat-scraping fug.

The way is firm underfoot and after crossing a well constructed footbridge the walker will be aware of some low mounds on the left hand side of the path. These are slag heaps. In no more than perhaps ten paces the remains of twenty bloomeries have been found, some dating back at least 1000 years. The walker may well find this hard to comprehend considering the scene today.

At the junction of paths at Low Birker, turn left and drop down to Doctors Bridge. Those staying at the Woolpack Inn or YHA should cross this bridge to join the walk from Penny Hill Farm to Hardknott. Doctors Bridge, so called because it was widened – look underneath at the change in stonework to allow the doctor to pass over in his dog cart.

Penny Hill Farm is a pretty place and the dogs will probably say hello as the walker passes through. Please make sure to shut the gates. The path is well marked and the way is through open pasture, then rising up a little along the fell edge through woodland and progresses through the occasional stream along the way to old mine workings across the way from Wha House Farm.

Penny Hill Farm has always considered itself to have been built on a Roman road; let us for a moment look at the terrain. The great stone slabs associated with the present Doctors Bridge probably indicate a possible good crossing point; however the river has swung around so much over the centuries and the field to the left of the track up to the farm suggest river bed and drained marsh.

Where did the Roman road go?

At Low Birker the dividing path allows access to Doctors Bridge and the valley bottom, or straight up the fell, but any idea of continuing along the contour is blocked by steep boulder fields. The whole hypothesis is open to debate because the track to Low Birker has the name New Church Lane; it trundles along through bloomery sites and charcoal burning areas connecting them together rather than taking a more militaristic A to B route. It suggests a route of post-Roman origin. Allowing for the topography and the general desire to keep feet dry the idea of the Roman road following the same route, above the marshy valley edge, is a sound one, but there

STAGE 3

seems to be a complete lack of remaining civil engineering features to prove it. Beyond Penny Hill farm things change.

From the shade of the wood, a near tunnel-like section, the path opens up on to the open fell. This section (just before the mine) shows considerable signs of effort in construction but then appears to peter out as it bears slightly right and reduces to a mere single-width track rounding an area of marshy ground. This open space suggests the remains of an ore processing area and seems to be built of the waste from the mine. In the summer the bracken makes the going uncomfortable if the walker strays off the path. The mine is well recorded; there is a shaft on the fell-side, however there are indications of earlier workings not associated with the shaft.

A short diversion up to the stark waste pile (the author has noted indications of lead as well as iron ore plus, quite unexpectedly, hints of copper!) brings the walker close to the steep drop to the falls. For the walker with children, supervision here is a must. Obviously common sense applies – the idea of going further along the path is risk fraught.

For the very careful adventurer it is possible to walk along the unprotected path that allows closer access to one of the mine entrances; glimpses of walls built into the right-hand side of the steep wet crevices make it very clear that, whilst the whole scene appears natural, man has been very hard at work here for a very long time.

Very recent investigations in the area above Wha House mine indicate a very significant archaeological find of potentially Roman origin, but that will have to wait for another day. The research to date does fill a gap in our understanding of the formal organisation and commercial exploitation of mineral extraction in the area.

Having crossed the beck, you will find that the route becomes a delightful narrow wandering path through woodland. The road is not far from the gaze. It is to the left of the path and lies partially beneath the stone wall line. The substantial remains of bridges lie just over the wall. They carry the road over the outflow from what must have been a waterfall on a grand scale, probably diverted to assist in the mining and processing of ore.

The stone wall is of note, being very well built and kept in good order. Wandering about, the present path passes the odd charcoal burner's platform, whilst the wall keeps to a regular contour, including some cutting work on the fell-side edge. This wall can afford the luxury

View over Eskdale.

of a direct route, as it has an earlier broader foundation to play with which becomes apparent when the next beck is reached, where time and nature has ploughed through the bridge. But by doing so, it has revealed a cross section of a well-constructed metalled road.

The walker can cross the beck with ease, when the weather is good, but a spot of rain can turn these trickles into torrents with ease. The path is in open steeply sided fell-side.

The author will admit he was initially nonplussed about where the road had gone from this point and it took nearly twenty years to find its course, and then it was just a lucky moment when the sun was at the right angle, the shadow just right and the vegetation just past its best. The latter could be said of the author – when in a moment of archaeological enlightenment he ploughed straight into waist-high bracken and fell over the edging stones holding the road in place on the steep grade, just at the point where the road (admitting defeat over the contour) eases its way down a little, but keeps itself out of the then mire of the valley bottom.

The walker should also note that the path has kept out of the bottom of the valley to the beginning of the pass over Hardknott. Although there have been attempts to drain the upper valley for in excess of seven hundred years, it was the economic depression of the 1930s that saw much of upper dale to the pass being tamed, as a means of finding useful employment for the unemployed. The river

STAGE 3

is now canalled and does as it is told, most of the time. Before these works the area was prone to flooding and the Latin name for the fort gives an indication of the conditions.

Middle bend in a river by a thicket.

The present path heads up the grade and through a kissing gate at which point the walker would expect a junction with the path over Harter Fell, but the grade is such that there is not.

The Harter Fell road is suggested as post Roman. However the practicalities of walking from A to B do not necessarily leave evidence of the builder and a route can be used, abandoned and re-opened many times over the centuries; it depends on the necessity of purpose at a particular moment. Certainly the route over, or more precisely, between the might of Harter Fell and Dow Crag has seen service in moving charcoal and it does point at a destination of Coniston Old Man, a scene of copper extraction from before the Romans, suggesting a potential reason for the route, but it does not indicate when and who built it.

Keeping to the Roman road (there you are – an archaeologist sticking a label on something!) is now relatively clear, with a well-constructed and well-drained surface following the wall line all the way to the present wire fence. A very short diversion through the next kissing gate and the present path comes in to meet the road as it takes a higher approach to the crossing of Hardknott Ghyll. The scene is an enjoyable one, save for the slight smell of brake pads, burning clutches and the din of first gears being engaged as motorists prepare for an extreme experience.

The walker has avoided the gate at the bottom of the pass, a short distance down to the left. Check if it's open or closed in the winter months and take note of any notice pertaining to conditions. There is a phone box and a call to the LDNP Weatherline on 0870 055 0575 would be sensible.

The walker is advised that from this point (Hardknott to Fold End) the route is a rigorous one; whilst it is on tarmac and therefore sound under foot (a disadvantage as there is no give) there are severe inclines and descents. Plan your trip carefully. This equally applies to those driving to locations along the way.

The way to Hardknott fort is instantly 'up', the air perfumed by

The long slog up Hardknott.

STAGE 3

burning brake pads and clutches. The present road zig-zags up the grade, but the Roman road, which can be discerned, goes straight up. Keep erosion to a minimum; grass has enough to cope with in these conditions, so stick to the road at this stage. Beware of the cars either trying the infamous Hardknott Pass route over to Ambleside or on the way down having completed the route. The coming down is worse than the going up.

Note that it is unclear where the Roman road actually starts. Whilst it is obvious as to the diversion off the tarmac on to the grass if the walker looks back, the origin is unclear. Is it the present road, down through the gate/grid, or to the left over the bridge and the path towards Wha House mine? The author considers both a possibility. This is not a case of hedging his bets, but a matter of practicality. The route straight down to the dale bottom would be useful for collecting reeds from the edge of the bog; a place for wildfowl, which would suggest hunting and snaring of game and quite possibly a ford using large punts across the open water at certain times of year connecting the way to the northern bank not far from the present modern bridge, where glacial and post glacial river erosion has provided a sill on which the road makes its way towards Boot. The potential seasonal nature of this way would suggest it is a minor, but nonetheless important connection. The other route, via Wha House mine, is the all-year-round one.

No doubt many historians will disagree and the author has broken his own rule by getting involved in the debate.

What does the walker think?

Opinions based on observation are always welcome. Feel free to add to the debate, but the walker should consider that the landscape has changed drastically in the last two thousand years and build that into the premise.

Back on the slog up Hardknott ...

Climbing the first steep grade soon ends and, not soon enough, the author tends to stop very regularly to make sure the view behind him has not changed. You never know that it might and that is his excuse and he is sticking to it – observation is essential, as is trying to breathe.

Taking a deep breath on this stretch means inhaling the last remains of somebody's clutch, so take care. Whilst not level, there is an ease of the grade for awhile, and at this point a signpost points the walker off the road to the left, pointing towards the fort. It should be noted that signs for the fort have been known to go missing and the wooden ones have provided the inconsiderate with kindling for camp fires, so check the map and bear left to the fort where you think appropriate. You will get wet feet. A clue is to bear left where the cars are parked – there are two appropriate locations. This still will not stop the walker from getting wet feet. Investigate at will and thoroughly for there is much to see.

The walker will be glad to be away from the road. The pass can be very busy, often with clusters of vehicles struggling in one direction, or the other, with the inevitable problems of meeting those going in the other direction. The walker can at least consider the strain of the grade less than the mental torture of trying to drive it. The walker can take his/her time; slow and sure and slow is the best way to tackle the next stage, but more anon.

This is an ideal location for dispelling most people's Metro Goldwyn Meyer impression of the Roman Empire and especially its legions. With the best will in the world the Roman road system over Hardknott and Wrynose cannot accommodate moving a legion in the manner oft portrayed – glistening parade armour, shields to the front, men marching at a steady pace heralded by officers and generals in the shadow of the imperial eagle. The reality would be very different. Trying to move a legion, which depending on the period of Roman history, could be up to sixteen thousand personnel, including doctors, clerks, officer slaves, wives, plus baggage train over such a pass would look somewhat less impressive and frankly impracticable. Whilst Hardknott is an auxiliary fort, it would have been constructed by the legions as was standard procedure in the Roman army, so at least a thousand skilled personnel struggled over the pass or worked their way up the dale to build it. But it seems unlikely that anything other than the title of legion ever passed this way again. Cohorts from legions and patrols most definitely did pass this way. Clad against the Cumbrian weather, with their ceremonial wear safely wrapped up in oil rags tucked under their bunks back in barracks, the mud attempting to penetrate the thick woollen socks trudging a well surfaced path, or cavalry walking their mounts to the summits looking forward to fodder and shelter – that would be the daily reality; the officers and legionary standards happily ensconced in the warmth of Ravenglass and Ambleside.

Having started early the walker gets the best of the air and has time to explore the fort. A short sharp way up the grade is to follow the Roman route which goes straight up rather than zig-zagging. The walker must at all times remember that this is a road, one which can genuinely terrify the driver, so steer clear of the cars as much as possible. It's also possible that you will overtake some and be joined by passengers, unexpectedly getting a chance to stretch their legs, lightening the load. Even in the age of lean-burn technically-advanced engines and gearboxes cars still come to grief on Hardknott on a regular if not daily basis.

The author remembers travelling down into Eskdale over the pass, when the car in front lost a wheel on a sharp bend. The occupants were less than happy about the experience!

"Welcome to Eskdale," was all we could think of saying as we helped rescue the occupants.

Golden Rule

Start Early
Plenty of fluids
Take your time
Keep to the present road if alone
Conserve energy (this is much steeper than you think)
Beware of traffic at all times

Hardknott Roman Fort

Mediobogdum

IMP CAES DIVI TRAIANI PARTHICI FIL DIVI NERVAE NEP TRAIANO
HADRIANO AVGVSTO PONT MAX ... COS III ... ... LEG AVG PR PR
COH IIII DELMATARVM FECIT

Have a look at the excellent information boards for the translation.
Hardknott in its commanding position overlooking Eskdale is an
example of Roman engineering set in a natural grandeur.

The fort lies a short walk off the present road. The going can be very
wet under foot, which is appropriate as the Bath House is the first of
the remains that come into view. No doubt a very welcome site to the
troops after a day tramping the fells! The walker should note that the
practicalities of the Roman Bath are all in place, but there is an air of
the utilitarian – Spartan in fact – in comparison with the bath at
Ravenglass. This is not just a case of the condition of preservation, but
the layout and feel of the place suggests a dark warm place with the
smell of sweat, peat and wood smoke in the air, amid the murmur of
voices easing cold bones. It has the sensation of squatness, of the need
to sacrifice grandeur for the understood desire for a refuge from the
wind and rain. The position of the Bath House near the eastern gate
gives some indication where the civilian settlement would be based. It
would difficult to consider a proper 'vicus' at Hardknott, but whilst the
fort was open, when the seasons allowed, the troops would require a
wide range of services – leather and metalworkers, wine, women and
the odd song as well! The walker should consider this landscape very
carefully as the remains of building bases can be clearly discerned.

From the Bath House to the fort is a short distance and it is simply
in the most commanding position, dominating the view down into
Eskdale and apparently blocking the way over the pass. The walker will
notice that there are piles of stone lying close to the fort; to us they
are just stone, but to the quarrymen who rebuilt the fort they were as
easy to read as a book.

There are excellent interpretation panels, but imagine and forget the
detail for a moment – just look at the view and dream. The layout of
the fort is quite clear and the outlines of some of the buildings are
obvious enough to give an impression of a bustling spot.

The word magnificent is often used regarding Hardknott. But this is

Hardknott from the Vicus.

The fort gates.

STAGE 3

Past glories revisited – Hardknott Roman Fort.

The slate line – stone above it is the rebuilt part.

The great walls of Hardknott Roman Fort.

The so-called parade ground.

The granary.

in the eye of the present, not the past. The fort is of standard Auxiliary design built a little after 119AD and the Latin scholars and classical historians among you will note that the inscription above (Cos III) relates to the fact that Hadrian was Consul for the third time in parallel with Publius Rusticus, and that the key date here is post-119AD, providing a baseline for construction. The reference to the third consulate is significant, under which Hadrian began reforms of the Army, allowing children of soldiers' rights of inheritance (permission to marry comes much later under Severus). The move must have been popular and as Dalmatia was a province controlled under pro-consular governor status, thus the LEG AVG PR PR, legatus Augusti pro prateore, the desire of the Dalmatian troops was obviously to be seen as part of the good works by a good emperor.

The fort inscription clearly identifies the inhabitants when it was new as Cohort IIII Dalmatians (from what is currently Bosnia-Herzegovina and Montenegro), so the troops would be at home in mountainous conditions and know something about sheep. The author considers the site of low military value – more a sheep station – for the administration of tax and provisioning of the army with wool and meat. The fourth (IIII) Dalmatia had been stomping around Britain since at least 103AD, according to a Roman military discharge diploma of that date included the cohort in its list of discharged personnel. Therefore it is quite possible that the Dalmatian forces had been deployed especially into the area for their skills observed in earlier campaigns – that of good mountain men.

Those wishing to consider the military strategic positioning of Hardknott will no doubt suggest that Hardknott acts as a block to anyone wanting to cross from west to east or vice versa. All well and good, and sounds fine and plausible, but let's put it to the test.

Consider an invading force, perhaps from north of the Hadrianic Wall. Should such an unfriendly force actually make it off the beach at Ravenglass, with intentions to head east, it would be met by forces from the fort at Ravenglass. Or, by good planning and not wishing to get a bloody nose from the first punch, the leader of such a force could attempt to bypass a beach assault by opting for an estuarine adventure up the river Esk. But this force would in turn come under surveillance and be attacked the moment it tried to come ashore.

Even if such a force did get through these trials and tribulations the bog below the fort would be enough to stop any army in its tracks and then, if there was sufficient planning and forces to overcome this obstacle, you would still have to climb Hardknott to face the Romans happily ensconced in wait to chuck rocks at you. Add to this that such an enormous number of enemy forces require months of planning to move, and that such would be just a tad obvious to the Romans well in advance of such attempted incursion and would therefore be in wait. It therefore seems unlikely that Hardknott really had much military importance.

Why and whom would be attempting it in the first place?

Try getting to the west from Wrynose would be equally suicidal – this is classic ambush territory. There are legends of Norse Army's coming to grief in Wrynose and there could be substance in the myths. The Kingdom of Northumbria was subjugated in 870AD and a puppet state under Viking control supplanted it with Ecgberht as king; however in 873AD Ecgberht and the Archbishop Wulfhere, fled along with part of the court and noble families. Whilst most fled south some appear to have crossed into West Cumbria and benefited from the fact they knew the terrain and locals. They seemed to have made themselves at home in Gosforth. Comfortable in the fact that they knew that any attempt to bring an army after them would fall foul of the terrain; an army of any size cannot operate well in the constricted environs of Wrynose.

In Roman times this route is a military backwater, a very unpleasant posting in early spring or autumn and frankly impossible in winter. There is no threat of invading armies – a bit of cattle and sheep rustling and defrauding the tax man maybe – but the terrain alone does not, nor would ever, see successful movement of hostile forces.

The author suggests that one of the reasons the remains of Hardknott are so intact is the fact it is of no military importance to anyone, it therefore gets left alone with no adaptations, no continuing use and no necessity to use it as a quarry (although the floor tiles seem to have migrated down into Eskdale in the 19th century), because it simply is so remote and off the map. The only people that passed over the pass for centuries were sheep herders and even they tended to avoid it.

The sheep might well be a clue. If anything, the so-called parade ground to the north east of the fort might well have more to do with stock holding and tax collection than a great military parade ground, or quite possibly both, as required. Open spaces for sheep or men, it is all a form of herding.

In fact from an archaeological perspective the area outside the fort is much more fun to explore, mostly because nobody has been much bothered to look at it. There are building platforms aplenty; the drainage system has survived in some spots, but not in others so watch out for a boot full. The Roman road out of the fort heading towards

Hardknott Contrasts.

Wrynose has survived, but it is the plethora of structure remains that capture the archaeologists' imagination, if not their trowels. Restored walls tell us little of the people that lived in this world. The every-day folk, their every-day existence, in this outpost of the Roman Empire are of the most interest.

A job unfinished.

Scudding clouds – time to leave Hardknott Roman Fort.

Like so many sites Hardknott is portrayed as a one-dimensional example of an Imperial age; there has been no attempt at understanding its context. The jigsaw shows the fort, but misses all the pieces that attach it to the people that lived in it.

As an Auxiliary fort, manned by the Roman Auxiliary troops, it is highly likely that Hardknott was also seen as a training camp after its first inhabitants, the Dalmatians (who would have loved it), departed – plenty of good steep fells and mountains, bracing conditions, especially if living out under canvas on the parade ground, turning raw recruits into hardened soldiers. The troops would be only too aware of the comforts at Ravenglass or Ambleside, only a day away at the very most – the bars, baths and houses of erotic delights. Instead these Auxiliaries

Hardknott – The Modern Frontier (for sheep).

STAGE 3

are stuck halfway up a mountain overlooking a festering midge-plagued bog chasing sheep.

All good character-building stuff, but not the stuff of daring do, or die.

Hardknott also has another rather unfortunate flaw – it is not at the top of anything, it is poised overlooking the Eskdale valley as it turns north east but it is overshadowed by the fell itself; it is very vulnerable from above.

In one important sense the fort at Hardknott is still serving one of the purposes it was undoubtedly built for, that of keeping the local population busy. Thousands of visitors visit the fort every year and Eskdale benefits from the trade, just as they always have done, servicing the troops in the past is servicing the tourists of today. Hardknott is justifiably the most important feature of the dale, all Imperial glory and bluster in its youth, with little true purpose; asleep for a thousand years in which the gilt and bluster has blown away on the wind and now truly serving the dale as a gentle wise old friend rather than a master.

How we Academics Lost a Golden Opportunity

STAGE 3

Many years ago the author was a volunteer on the Ravenglass & Eskdale railway, alongside a member of the railway staff who had been in the dale for most of his adult life, working on the railway and the associated quarry at Beckfoot. Back in the 1950s the quarry company was taken over by another organisation, with intentions of crushing the granite for concrete to be used in the construction of Calder Hall nuclear power station. Unfortunately there was a flaw in the plan, because the granite was too radioactive. The quarry was thus surplus to requirements and was closed. The workforce was on the dole, but fortunately not for long – their skills were to be used by the Ministry of Works restoring Hardknott Fort. The workforce were all experienced quarry men, knowing exactly how rock works, how stone fits on stone and they duly just picked up the stones and put them back where they belonged. (Visitors will see, if they look closely enough, that there is a layer of slate identifying what was standing and what was rebuilt.) The work progressed very well indeed – too well.

"It wasn't difficult work, we just picked it up like we would any other wall and put it back, but the buggers wouldn't let us finish it. We knew exactly how to finish it."

Simply majestic view from Hardknott.

STAGE 3

Which means that because the archaeologists and academics considered the workforce only labourers and not craftsmen, and because the academics had no idea what the top of any Roman fortification actually looked like because none had remained from ancient times and what had survived from documents was unclear as

Another majestic View from Hardknott at dusk.

to actual detail, the academics were unwilling to take the risk of ridicule from their peers. "Good Lord, they're only labourers for heaven's sake."

The result of which we; lost a golden opportunity of knowing exactly what the top fortifications on a Roman fort, or Hadrian's Wall for that matter, actually looked like.

All because the academics knew best. Do we ever learn?

But enough of the detail – the walker should stop thinking for awhile, and just look. Let the modern world melt away. It's all here. Just let it reveal itself again.

The view from the fort is stunning – down to the sea. The walker can now imagine what the view looked like two thousand years ago – much more silver glinting the eye, the mystical smoke from charcoal burning, spears of light from a distant patrol heading down to Ravenglass disturbing the ducks that fly across the bow of the craft heading past what is now the George IV Inn. Add another five metres to the highest remaining wall and the panorama would widen even further, but only to the west. The compass is blocked by the weight of the fells.

Having enjoyed Hardknott Fort and environs there is still a veritable mountain to climb and there is no route but the road up to the present summit so the tarmac does tend to bounce off the soles of the boots and in hot weather the grade becomes taxing in the extreme.

The walker should take time – this is the most taxing stretch because there is nowhere but the road and it is constantly up. Stop where safe to do so and enjoy. Enjoy a lot as it is magnificent, wild and a tad dangerous which the walker will feel the higher and deeper into the pass he/she treads. The walker will understand why nobody crossed the passes, other than the odd shepherd (sheep again) and why it was avoided at all cost. It is not just that it is physically tough-going and when you reach the top you see how far you yet have to go, it's the atmosphere. It can be exhilarating, enlightening and in a moment sheer hell. There is nowhere to hide and it's just the walker and the moment, usually very wet, very cold and utterly sapping. Just be aware that the fells permit you through and there is often a price to be paid for this cursory tolerance.

To the left of the present summit there is reasonable evidence of the Roman road trundling along on its own course, its ditches clogged. It is surprisingly wet underfoot even on a dry day; elsewhere the scenery demands that there is nowhere else for the road to go than the present route, so for once the evidence of Roman activity is absolute, the walker is on Roman ground and can be thankful for the skilful engineering involved. Stop regularly to enjoy the view back down into

STAGE 3

Eskdale and beyond to the sea and Ravenglass. The summit is not one where you can see both views at once, not on foot at least; provided it is not raining or blowing a gale there are plenty of places to rest up and watch the cars go by, if the walker can see them through the low cloud! Congratulations, the walker is now at 393 metres above sea level and at the highest part of the walk.

It is at the summit, slightly on the Wrynose side, that a path trundles off down to Black Hall, considered to be Roman by some, discounted by others, and sometimes known as the 'Lead Road' (which might give the game away as to its purpose). However, the fact it climbs all the way up a very steep grade and then down the other, rather than taking a slightly easier route between Harter fell and Dow Crag suggests an urgency of purpose. The route over Hardknott cannot be described as an enjoyable one (the walker should consider that the pleasure of enjoying the scenery without industrious purpose is less than two hundred years old), especially when exposed to the elements, and it is acknowledged that few other than sheep herders would attempt it, for fear of being caught out in the extreme weather conditions that are possible on the passes. This would make it ideal for a smuggling route for which Ravenglass was, for a while, most heartily employed in the business. Very few revenue men would attempt to intercept illicit goods via Hardknott.

The walker, suitably filled with the odd car fume, can now start the

The old road to the Hardknott summit is on the left.

The prospect ahead – Hardknott Pass, from the fort site.

Wrynose, looking east from Hardknott Pass.

STAGE 3

The western bastions. Simply glorious.

The approach to Wrynose.

dramatic descent towards Cockley Beck and Wrynose Pass. There is little doubt, allowing for the modernisation of the road by addition of a bit of tarmac and the odd new bridge (replacing those damaged by the weight of British Army lorries in WWII), that the course is the same as the Roman. The walker will note a few alterations, but in general can be well satisfied that they are tramping along the route just as the Romans did, except they didn't have to watch out for cars, which can be a full time occupation if the walker hits the descent mid afternoon during the peak of summer. Some of the drivers will be doing the route because it's there. Others by mistake, because it appears and is the fastest route on paper, or advised by GPS, between the Central Lakes and the far west. The expertise of one driver is undone by the novice in front, so it can be well worthwhile walking with eyes in the back of the walker's head.

Many years ago the author worked in the booking office at Dalegarth, Boot, station and would be asked twenty odd times a day for an alternative route back as the ashen-faced drivers couldn't face the prospect. It still happens to this day.

On the lower slopes the route begins to vary a little from the Roman, partially because of erosion, and the author has spent considerable hours researching the possibility of a formal Roman structure at Cockley Beck. The location would suggest a need to marshal troops and have a rest station before or after the climb in either direction. The

Tough on the ankles: the descent towards Cockley Beck.

water supply is also useful and the definite need for warm shelter in case of adverse conditions makes the hypothetical scenario more like a possibility. It's just a case of working out where it is?

From the air there is clear indication that there was a formal junction of Roman roads on the Hardknott side of the beck, with a road heading through from the direction of Broughton via Broughton Mills and Newfield, but that is for another day; let the walker enjoy a few moments taking in the view, the scale of the landscape. The author notes that this junction is virtually impossible to see on the ground as a result of centuries of flash floods and erosion.

Wrynose gentle approach.

A magnificent bridge at Cockley Beck.

Another view from the opposite side.

Those walkers walking the route alone should keep to the road through the pass and should cross the road bridge. The river Duddon runs relatively wide and fast – a noisy river across the valley bottom – and if a lone walker gets into difficulty on the opposite side from the road it is hard to catch someone's attention.

Do Not Expect Your Phone To Work Here!

Cockley Beck farm is a private house, where there is a phone box that many in Cumbria fought hard to save and has proved a vital lifeline. The author urges the walker to support the retention of these essential services wherever they may hove from.

Those following the Roman road along its actual course should bear left before the Cockley Beck road bridge and bear left keeping the river Duddon on the right. Look out for a magnificent Cumbrian slab bridge which will save you from getting your feet wet. This is located over the

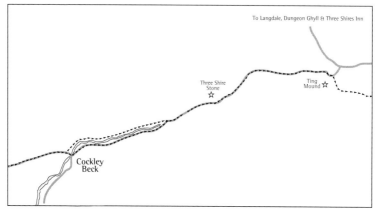

stile, otherwise it's a boot full of ice cold water. There are numerous building bases close to the present bridge on the Hardknott side suggesting that Cockley Bridge was once much larger than it is today. This should come as no surprise – the route would have required some formal management. Additional pack animals need fodder and shelter, plus repair of boots and harnesses and the need to quench the thirst before, or after the journey would suggest a vibrant community, now long gone.

This route will involve crossing fast flowing water. If the becks are running fast do not venture along the old road. Take the modern one for the way under foot will otherwise be punctuated with wetness and an un-fordable beck at the far end.

Taking to the old Roman road offers a wonderful view and experience on a good day, and with minor becks cutting through the road it is possible to deduce its construction. There are some interesting

Cockley Beck.

STAGE 3

The way to the Roman Road, Wrynose. Not for the solitary traveller and those not wishing to get wet feet.

field works along the way and the area by the old abandoned farm buildings; this is part of the Gaitscale complex (the word is carefully chosen) and there are several key structures in the area deserving further investigation by archaeologists' future. One aspect to consider is its position, approximately half way between the two passes – a geographical significance and a shelter for travellers in either direction, plus a rest point for horses.

Above the ruins is the ancient complex sheep enclosure that reminds the author of the Romano British settlement at Brotherswater; there are echoes of layout, both for enclosure of stock and habitation. All around are the remains of patches of well worked land now lying idle. The author has walked the fields and there are signs, further up the slope, of enough structural remains to suggest a relatively large settlement with one large formal building now divided by a much later boundary wall.

Wrynose

The Author bids, as is his wont, the walker to look beyond the obvious and seek the past, so close to hand.

In military terms there can hardly be a more difficult passage than that between the heights of Wrynose and that of Hardknott. The valley offers no highland route between the passes; the valley floor offers the only way for any formal road to traverse the scene.

This factor is wholly significant in the dating of the Roman road. It

*Cockley Beck.
Sweaty-palm time
for drivers.*

STAGE 3

must date from a period of stability and peace, and no such formal works can have been undertaken unless the Romans had complete and utter control of the entire fell system in all directions. Construction and operation would have been impossible. The opportunity of blocking the route and throwing rocks is all too easy to accomplish.

However, the possibility that the route was a well-trodden one, before the Romans, must be taken into account. The geography is the key. The fells give way just enough to allow a relatively easy passage on foot. The dip in the fell chain is just enough to entice the explorer and

A site in need of investigation in Wrynose Pass.

A dry day in Wrynose.

The Ancient Pass, looking back from the east. The watercourse points the way to Hardknott.

traveller alike. It is therefore likely that the route was well trodden before Roman engineers got to grips with formal improvements.

The passes presented no difficulties to the Roman engineers, accomplished at Roman road construction through the Alps; this Cumbrian terrain was no more than a blip to them. The most difficult part of the engineering would have been the constant flow of water off the fells and the seasonal changes in that flow. Dry beds in the summer turning to torrents in winter, ably constrained in well built culverts – these, over the centuries, through the lack of a tending hand, have deteriorated and the road is demolished by the hands of nature and time. But through this destruction, a cross-section of the construction technique is clear to see.

Contrary to common belief, there is no single Roman road method, as the author has mentioned elsewhere; the circumstances and available material are key factors. In this case the temptation to use virgin river-bed stone is to be scorned, being too round, offering little or no abrasion, no unification of purpose and no holding hands with the next stone to make a good compact surface. The bed shows sign of charcoal and a light dusting of iron ore, not an uncommon finding, as the marker or tracing for the exact location of the road, set down by the surveyor's team to be followed by the heavy engineering crew. Then there's a layer of fine smashed river cobble with fine granite gravels compacted with larger horizontally laid flat cobble atop of which is another layer of fine gravel with a higher sand content, with ore and granite gravels. The edging is a formal stone culvert along most of the fell side edge, this feature being a necessity to deal with the constant threat of inundation. Indeed, when built, the road would have stood proud of the surrounding landscape, rising above the river and attendant agriculture.

The scene of desolation, of fractured space and empty majesty, is not the scene of the Roman gaze. Whilst the fells are ever present, the small field systems and road side farm and inn, come refuge against the storms, would be a more welcoming sight. A hunk of bread, cheese and oysters all topped off with a mug of local brew would ease the traveller and fill the locals' pockets with much needed income. While we, the traveller, see perfection in the nature of place, our forefathers saw a practicality that we have lost, a need to make sense and purpose, to harness and understand what could be made straight and to a better use. Today we walk easy, without a heavy load. We do not carry for trade, we carry for pleasure. There would have been much trade in pack animals and cart repairs, horses requiring attention, extra equipment

STAGE 3

STAGE 3

Coming Down Wrynose.

required, fodder and foodstuffs – plenty to make this still scene hum with life. The walker should stop, listen beyond the sound of the beck and hear for the past that in this distant place is closer, more tangible, by the lack of today permeating the air. Listen for the road gang complaining about the use of heavy carts on the road damaging the culverts, the swearing fracas as sheep and their herders meet a Roman cohort making its way to Hardknott, the blacksmith hard at his anvil scorching bright, tantalised by the silver sound of ale to jug and convivial company in raucous song.

Join the happy company for a moment and let time slip as a second to a thousand years beyond your grasp. Visit a humanity that once was in such a place – not lost, just beyond our sight. Such is Wrynose, a place of laughter and life. Beware its nature when it blasts, but revel in its hidden beauty.

The fell-bound path continues away from the road over the tops to Seatoller and on to Keswick – a route in operation thousands of years before the Romans. In the opposite direction the ancient way appears to head towards Coniston, so this group of buildings stands testament to a continual stream of travellers. The weather is doing its very best to pull the stones apart and most travellers on the main road will not give the spot a second glance, much as the shepherds passing the Roman fort in days gone by – a place of no significance to their present day. It is always the apparently insignificant that proves to be quite the opposite.

The author is a professional archaeologist and is well used to the usual opening gambit of a visitor to an excavation. The archaeologists can be a metre or two below present ground level. Various masonry remains will be apparent, a scattering of pottery and some skeletal remains will be being worked upon – and the visitor will always invariably say...

..."Have you found anything yet?"

To which, through years of practice the author will quite honestly reply in the affirmative, but then produce the smallest item of finds possible (charcoal is best). The audience is normally somewhat subdued. A little black smudge will suffice – it is in many cases much more significant than all the rest put together, because within it lies a date. From the charcoal, with radiocarbon dating, a time span is produced – something to hang all the rest on; an axis point on which to revolve the hypothesis about the rest of the site. This is the same with hordes of coin – it is not the coin that really interests, it is the container in which they lay that sparks the most interest from an archaeologist. So, a few bumps in the ground can mean a lot.

STAGE 3

Keep an eye on the weather and certainly watch the path. The road can be traced throughout the bottom of the pass, but care must be taken crossing some of the streams that cut across the route. The walker is reminded to keep to the designated route on the Ordnance survey map and will note that the remains of the road peter out, the evidence wiped clean from the landscape on the north side, and the walker needs to cross the sometimes torrent to the modern road. Cross the official 'DIY' stile, the top horizontal foot plank spending most of its life not attached to the two uprights, which makes for an interesting balancing act when crossing the fence line. Do not attempt to continue eastward on the north side as it becomes a slide and is an uncomfortable experience and is not on a recognised route, nor is it the road as it has crossed to the south side; the bridge now long gone and in the torrents of winter all trace will have been eradicated long ago. The walker might like to suggest where it might be. Based on the landscape and the evidence for the road on both sides of the beck the construction would have had to take the extreme weather conditions into accounts, there being no shortage of material to build the structure. Where can it be?

From 393 metres at Hardknott summit the walker has descended to 218 metres, then back up to 393 metres for the Wrynose summit, which makes the going relatively easy across the Wrynose valley bottom. The Roman road, having spent at least half of the length of the valley on the north side, transfers to the south. The author knows several motorists who quite categorically state they know when they are on the Roman road because the quality of the ride improves. The author has no reason to disbelieve them.

Use common sense and ford where you consider shallow. Most of this stretch is normally no more than a boot and sock-soaking high. The boulders do move and the current can be strong so take it easy. If in doubt, work your way back to Cockley Beck and cross by the bridge and put it down to experience and research.

Why ruin an adventure by breaking your ankle or neck?

Once crossed, the tarmac of the present road takes over; beneath is the Roman road and the short sharp rise up to the summit commences. It's still steep but easier than Hardknott. This is a slog, but there is

The old road veers away to the left.

Welcome to a land of adventure.

much to see and more importantly the way is slightly more open from the perspective of cars and walkers meeting; room for both to co-exist.

Welcome to Three Shires Stone at 393 metres. It's an enjoyable spot and undoubtedly a stopping point for all travellers down the ages. Three shires? Because this was the County boundary for Cumberland, Westmorland and Lancashire; 'those were the days' – the stone survives and nothing else, the territory now being Cumbria. However the fact that this was an agreed territorial boundary does have significance historically and it is at this point many fell routes meet.

STAGE 3

A gentle beck a torrent makes.

Archaeologically more research needs to be undertaken in the surrounding environs.

Three Shires stone sits above Widdygill and all around the walker will be aware of glacier moraine with ridges and mounds scarring the scene. The walker can investigate the scene, as any good archaeologists should, and ponder if all the mounds are the work of nature, or of man, or perchance man improving upon that of nature to improve the view, or bury the dead. Such ponderings are good for the resting of the feet and best carried out in the company of others and a bottle of ale to refresh the postulations. But the walker must note that there is some way to go before the pass is really cleared and whilst a rest and postulation is advised, do not let the scene seduce, as the road down towards Langdale is the only way if the walker is to keep to the approximate Roman route, and there are more cars on this route than most would expect from such a remote location.

"I find the weather often changes significantly when crossing the old County boundaries." John Buckland

STAGE 3

Some motorists, emboldened from their experience of Langdale and after escaping its relatively gentle clutches via a 'nursery' fell road route, feel that the fells cannot possibly offer a greater challenge; others

Heading down to the Langdales.

because it was the shortest route on the map; others deliberately doing the route because it is there.

The author has often noted that the cars head up the fell in little pack horse trains, seeking out the relative safety of knowing other foolhardy souls are about to undertake the assault – plus the opportunity of a witness to the success, or a helping hand to pick up the pieces, is undoubtedly never out of the motorists' minds!

Most motorists end up in the same state, suddenly aware that nature is mightier than they and all the technology and power in the world, in the hands of an amateur, is but a waste.

To the walker, the danger (for danger there is), is the grim determination shown by the motorist, oblivious to the walker, the sweat pouring from the brow, the steering wheel bulging under the pressure of hands clutched in a deathly embrace – passengers suddenly aware that the predicament is not such a jolly one as first considered sit in mute silence awaiting the inevitable. This combination leads to blindness of purpose, for everything else around is secondary to survival, or so it seems, the author having more than once having to leap (an activity outside the parameters of the author's strict lack of serious exercise regime) out of the way of vehicles on the road. Three

STAGE 3

The old road Wrynose is not recommended!

Shires Stone is oft a point for turning back, so the walker has as many opportunities for cars that have been dodged coming up the way to attack from behind less than twenty minutes later, in rapid retreat.

The walker should note that when walking down the road towards Fell Foot they should be very careful of stepping off the road to the right, which will be obvious once on the walk. The Wrynose Beck falls away fast into Widdygill Foot, from whence the River Brathay is born and the opportunity of getting a closer look by stepping off the edge is to be avoided by the likely rate of descent.

Towering to the walker's left is Hollin Crag and the descent through this stretch in inclement weather can provide impromptu and spectacular waterfalls down its face. Past Pedder Stone, reputedly the rest point for those crossing the pass, but more likely a boundary point for the Ting Mound that the walker will pass at Fell Foot. Pedder Stone sits, not quite, but close enough, between Three Shires Stone and the Ting Mound. Whilst the three Counties are a modern invention in historical terms, the need for territorial boundaries based on the geography of the area is clear enough and whilst the present boundary marker is much later than the Ting Mound in political terms, the three major trackways converge (as previously described) in a significant meeting point of the pre Roman period.

A Ting Mound is a meeting place; these appear throughout northern Europe and appear to be an iron age institutionalised area of meeting for dispute settling. These 'settlement' zones appear to survive the Romans into the early medieval period and in some cases survive to this day as market squares, often still with ancient stones attached as markers as to the boundary of tolerant debate.

In this instance the Ting Mound sits within the eastern territory, but

Marker stones in Wrynose.

within clear view of the western and cannot be deemed to be advantageous militarily from an army bearing down on it from above, it is partially hidden by a bluff, which the present road passes under the shadow of Castle Howe to Fell Foot. It cannot be described as a defendable site. Its role suggests that it must in fact be open and exposed.

A reason for the author to consider the Pedder Stone as a significant boundary?

If a dispute is to be settled by debate all parties must agree an area where no force will be used, to allow for a par lei. Consider such a situation where a party from the west has agreed to meet a party from the east. The eastern party waits at the Ting Mound; those from the west can be seen descending the fell, the glint of weapons and shield bosses and set against the fell backdrop can be seen from afar. The western party, stopping at the Pedder Stone offers the eastern party some acknowledgment that those from the west are willing to par lei. Rather than if they descended non-stop, even with good intentions, this could easily be construed as a war party descending pall mall on to those from the east. So a stopping place it is, but with a deeper purpose than resting the feet.

STAGE 3

Having dodged the motor cars the walker can, between such onslaughts, continue down the grade. Not much further down the way is a footpath to Blea Moor Tarn, a useful route to Dungeon Ghyll.

Take this path if you have booked accommodation in Dungeon Ghyll or at the National Trust campsite. Dungeon Ghyll is the terminus of the bus service to Ambleside and beyond – check the timetable in advance. The walk is a very reasonable one but always consider it further than you think, with considerable ascent and descent, especially at dusk. A good pace is needed.

This is followed by another footpath that cuts across to the road for Dungeon Ghyll, which can be a tad wet under foot as it crosses Blea Moss, so take the first which keeps things dry and keeps you off the road. The scenery is dramatic with the land dropping away as if in a hurry to get to the Ghyll.

Under Castle Howe, on the left, the road bears sharp right to Fell Foot farm, where the farm allows the road passage past its front door.

The road to Dungeon Ghyl.

The farm has excellent accommodation, but be sure to book in advance. Access to the Ting Mound is via the farm. Remember to shut the gate and take note of the sign.

Interestingly Castle Howe has signs of a building foundation on its top; it is considered both "Medieval" and "Uncertain", which covers most of the bases, whereas the real answer would to put a spade in the ground and find out. The author suspects it is earlier than medieval (unless referring to early medieval which is really about 500-800AD – the dark ages are rightly being extinguished as more research reveals a highly complex post-Roman world) and maybe associated with the Pedder stone and the Ting Mound, which is how the author came up with his possible hypothesis.

For the walker not stopping at the farm, or Dungeon Ghyll, the journey to Three Shires Inn via the road is a fast one, but not a comfortable experience at certain times of day – again beware the cars. The author suggests preventing further contact with the motor car and that a more enjoyable route is called for, but recognises the need to get to a place of warmth and comfort, not forgetting a pint of good ale! So the walker should speed on before nightfall.

The Three Shires Inn is a smashing place to stay. A warm friendly welcome awaits, with good beer, food, beds and company. Book in advance or be disappointed. For those not shattered by the day's activities there are plentiful short walks from here, but the author suspects the best walk will be to the Slaters Bar!

The Three Shires Inn.

Stage Four

A good stretch of the legs with plenty of contrast, to Ambleside

Whichever spot the walker has decided to use for an overnight stop, the walk continues from Fell Foot Bridge and crosses the Greenburn Beck.

The walker will have desired much rest after the crossing of the passes and can be relieved by the fact that the way and landscape is gentler in nature from now on. The views will have warmed the soul, if the weather has been kind, or reminded the walker of the fragility of existence, if not.

Those staying in Dungeon Ghyll must allow time to get back to Fold End in respect of their walking day.

The author is aware that some believe the Roman road heads into Dungeon Ghyll and Great Langdale. There is no doubt to believing that there was a proper route through the dale, pre-dating the Romans and no doubt improved by them, but the author considers the options for the most direct route between Ravenglass to Ambleside to be (very roughly) a straight line; the route via Great Langdale is a diversion, and a very profitable one if mining was being undertaken, but that is commerce and the military would have other priorities.

The key to the possible location of the Roman road from Fell Foot to Ambleside is the landscape; the farm sits on the edge of a drained bog which would in turn once have been a lake; the remains of which are Little Langdale Tarn. The walker should take a close look at the map for the area and note that all the paths keep well away from the tarn and effectively stay on the 110m contour; this is no coincidence. Anyone wanting to travel west has to work either side of this open water and,

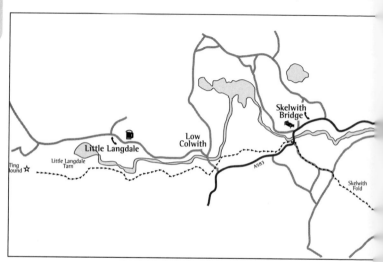

Colwith force.

like Eskdale, there is probably a need for two types of route, one local for hunting, grazing and provisioning and another all year-round route for communication. This would suggest that the Roman road turned sharp right by Castle Howe, followed the 120m contour, over the river Brathay, then over the Greenburn Beck and joined with the track from Fell Foot Bridge Farm at Bridge End. Field research suggests that there are indeed remains of a way along this contour and some of the field boundaries take it into account, suggesting that it stayed in operation long after the Romans left and as long as the land was not drained there would have been little choice. The track from Fell Foot to Bridge End is a relative modern one and would have been more than a tad wet in the past. There are some fascinating field systems and ancient walls along this section identifying an attempt to get a high productivity out of land relatively recently drained; the shapes seem to indicate a progression of clearance, every bit of land gained and worked in turn with the walls following the effort to identify individual ownership or responsibility for the individual shapes are probably the key, like a signature.

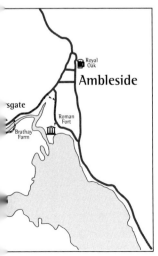

STAGE 4

A diversion to Cathedral cave is a must on this section of the walk but must be undertaken at the walker's own risk, as the sign on the entrance clearly states. It is a wonder of Cumbria, a mixture of the efforts of man and the healing hand of nature – an elemental place where light is precious, where the unexpected happens. A drop of ice-cold water opens the fragile places within, where the darkness is soul-less; a place of mysterious personal exposure; frightening

Back on the track, the walker cannot be mistaken in thinking this is truly magnificent scenery. Knott Head looms above and the way underfoot is good, in fact very good indeed with good reason, the path heading for the quarry near Atkinson Coppice.

Interestingly, there are the remains of a lime kiln within the coppice; who built it and when, nobody knows. There you are – some research for you! We archaeologists don't know everything. Anybody can do research and get involved with the past.

Tarmac. Parts of this route are in fact well-surfaced road. However, the walker should note for the most part the walk isn't on it.

The Roman way is slightly further down the slope than the present track and keeps to the lower contour which the walker will rejoin as they drop down from the quarry towards Slater Bridge, a very obvious reminder of the occupation of those six days a week all around.

The Three Shire Inn is on the opposite side of the bridge, a short

Colwith Bridge sunshine day.

A well-metalled way.

A rural way in need of investigation.

walk along a well marked way. Those starting today from the inn may curse the author for the round trip, but the purpose is to explore and get as much of the original route under boot as possible.

Continuing along the path the river comes into close contact with the truly ancient ford for the passage of the Langdale stone axes out of Langdale, through Tilberthwaite, Coniston and Broughton out to the Irish Sea. The axe factories in Langdale date from 3400BC giving a proper sense of time and industrial perspective to the landscape. The path then takes us across the rise to Stang End where there is good evidence of a well-built road, date unknown.

The walker soon meets with Colwith Force; the sound attracts the walker off the road and down the bank – in fact the sound can be quite tremendous and Colwith Force is often heard before seen. If, as the author thinks, the Romans would have reverentially built a shrine or two in niches, for the Romans were enchanted by the sound of water and listened for the gods to speak to them through the medium. If you sit by the outer edges of the force the ground shakes and the boulders and pebbles sing a deep musical melody to this day.

The walker needs to climb back up to the track, minding the slippery steps and turn left to continue the traverse. The Roman road is at this point about to take a sharp right turn. The path will take you down a well-marked track through a cutting; as the walker descends the cutting begins to take an embankment into account on the right, the

Course of Roman road...

present track being to the left in what was the ditch. The road prepares to cross what is now a stream by means of a bridge, and taking the geography into account this is probably the first Colwith Bridge, long before the marshy ground below was cleared. The present crossing of the stream is an easy one and the way beyond can be muddy underfoot for a short section until the next well-bridged stream and the junction of two ancient roads, one coming up the pass from Coniston on the right and the way the walker is treading, to the left the way to Skelwith. This is a well-constructed and maintained road which appears to have survived until the early nineteenth century. The road is a footpath and brings the walker out onto the present Colwith Bridge road. The walker should turn left and note on the right that the old road continues across the modern one into the bushes, before taking a series of

STAGE 4

Road goes straight on. Path turns right. Please keep to the path..

...and farther on.

dramatic zig-zags and then a majestic contour alignment to climb the hill. Alas this is on private property. The walker should descend the present road and then turn right over the stile on to the present path.

The walker is about to encounter two Roman road systems meeting with significant remains, only one is on public rights of way and the other lies on privately-owned land. Needless to say their discovery has caused many sleepless nights as they too hold mysteries and as usual pose as many questions as answers. But, they do both take particular interest in the landscape; they keep well out of the wet, or what was wet when they were built. This is a significant factor throughout the walk – keeping troops dry under foot is a wise precaution, whereas wagon wheels actually need some wet to keep them together, the wood requiring regular swelling to keep the rim integrity.

The walker must stay on the Cumbria Way past Low Park, Park Farm and on to Park House. This is really enjoyable walking, but often busy, especially at weekends and in the summer holidays as the path connects Colwith to Skelwith and the author has often been impressed by the standard of walking equipment, with the price tags just snipped off (and occasionally not), of the walkers squeaking their new boots between the two falls. At first glance the casual observer would not accept this track, often a very narrow and bumpy way, that connects these spots, as post-Roman and certainly not a road. Initially the author had much to mutter about on this section, considering that the road may well lie beneath the present A593. But diligent research proved that whilst the present way is in places challenging, there is clear evidence of the original road in place.

STAGE 4

The old road.

Enjoy the scenery, but the Roman road is indeed with the walker. It's just a case of spotting it.

Having crossed the stile and made it up the steps to the cliff edge the walker will soon realise that the first part of this section is modern, a route along the river bank, effectively the way across the meadow at the start would be under water probably less than two hundred years ago. The Roman road has kept to higher ground and faced with the climb has made the way up the slope in gracious style, unlike the present path.

The walk to Skelwith is a well trodden one, well marked and with a motorway standard rambling surface in parts. However, walkers should take care on the stretch immediately above the wooden steps at the start of this section. This section of path is narrow and very dangerous and is in need some attention. Whilst the author doesn't believe in making the world into a piece of cotton wool, he does consider that if a path is to be upgraded, as this one has for most of its length, it wouldn't be a bad idea to stop this bit from falling over a very precipitous cliff, which is undoubtedly the direction the unhappy walker will take with it! SO BEWARE!!!

The route, soon released from mortal peril, is then across open fields, gently climbing up the contours (a setting quite suitable for a Julie Andrews "the hills are alive" moment). The road is the other side of the rise at this point, avoiding the warbling (the present path is a new one), on private land. The author muses as to the effect Julie Andrews would

A fine site – Skelwith Bridge Hotel and Talbot Pub.

have had on the Ninth Legion and whether this was the reason for its disbandment! Suddenly dragged back to near reality and by sharp contrast, the walker is squeezed along property lines and at the very best could be seen as an agricultural way, allowing access to fields and the next farm. However this is the course of the road or, to be precise, the very edge of it. The present way between farms retains the essential core of the road, and while the path meanders all over the place, there are traces of the earlier, more formal way still in place; difficult to find but they are there. The author will not spoil the picture – this section is wonderful, varied and good underfoot. There is even a junction with another road, clearly delineated and the author muses that it is heading for a villa, taking advantage of the military way and its opportunity for easy communication, much like the Victorian newly rich with their 'brass castles' and the steam age.

It takes little to convince the walker that, whilst they are not marching along a straight well defined Roman road, the consolation is more than worthy. Much praise should be heaped on those for their efforts to maintain this stretch.

Light woodland glades provide shade and only the A593 creates a stir to remind the walker of modernity.

There is an exceptional remain of the road a short distance from the junction with the A593. The author challenges the walker to find it!

Skelwith Force is a delight, early in the day before the arrival of the tourists and especially immediately after a night of rain. With only a

STAGE 4

four-metre drop it is not a grand cascade, but the water punches through with bravado.

The author has researched the area beyond Park House and considers the path from there towards Skelwith Bridge, that effectively parallels the modern A593, to be the possible course of the Roman road, not right down to the bridge itself, but crossing on a higher contour across the present A593 at an oblique angle a little to the left of the turning for Skelwith Fold. The bridge replaced a ford; this would never have done for the Romans and the author does not believe the Romans crossed the river at the present bridge site. However, as the bridge is available and there being a fine Inn – to be precise The Talbot Bar – at Skelwith Bridge Hotel it is worthy of the walker's attention.

Having refreshed, the walker may contemplate the day so far. The territory has been a curious one from delightful open vistas, with reasonable walking under foot, some magical, mysterious settings, Cathedral Cave full of darkness and ferns, Colwith and Skelwith Force bursting with energy. But, apart from a couple of short stretches the Roman world seems completely lost. Fear not, the adventure is in the discovery. There is much to be done between Fold End and Skelwith Bridge – why not start that research and let the author know what you have found?

The walker should re-cross Skelwith Bridge and turn left down the B-road to Skelwith Fold. This takes the walker up and out of the wet

STAGE 4

Skelwith Bridge.

around Skelwith and is soon joined by the Cumbria Way that does not take a diversion to the Talbot Bar. It has kept to the slightly higher contour, as does the Roman road. The walker will cross the Roman road shortly after the junction and there is some indication of its route as it crosses the field to the walker's left. The road then rejoins the walker on the approach to Skelwith Fold where it crosses the present way, making its final accent effectively through the back gardens of the houses.

The road is heading for Ambleside. But not without a subtle twist in the route, but with good reason as will become apparent.

This is good walking through deep hidden ways where the sunshine is mottled and ripples with the leaves. At the Y-junction bear left, up the steep bit into the settlement proper. The walker will undoubtedly be astonished by the magnificent modern houses intermingled with some wonderful Cumbrian vernacular gems. Skelwith Fold is hidden away, as the walker will have noted by the width of the road, and likes to keep it that way. Bear right at the junction, then, within a very short distance turn left on to the track, marked with a footpath sign.

The author will allow that the present footpath is as close as possible to the original route as allows at this point.

It should come as no surprise that the area around Skelwith Fold has seen charcoal burning activity, the woods having been coppiced thoroughly over the centuries, with flat stone based platforms dotted about. The older properties nestle in tight formation at the junction. Whilst Skelwith Fold appears to be a dead village it is in fact alive and kicking with strenuous efforts to keep the community spirit going. If you see the donation box spare a few bob for a good cause.

Out of Skelwith Fold and starting the descent the walker can truly enjoy the scene. This is classic Lake District walking and downhill too, which is always enjoyable after a bit of up. One of the first notable features is the remains of quarry workings, not a new sight for the walker, but usually associated with good going under foot. The track the walker is traversing is no doubt associated with these workings and Skelwith Fold would have housed the workforce, but the origins of this quarry require further research. Easy descent for materials in many directions but mainly, the author suspects, down towards the mere.

This footpath, whilst serving quarrying at the Skelwith Fold end trundles past the quarry and begins its descent towards the lake and more precisely the B5286 and Pull Wyke.

Cumbrian man has hacked away at Mire Side Hill with good effect. Just as with Cathedral Cave earlier in the day, the effort of men is always staggering. Fortunately to the left the tree line of Beckmire Rigg and Holme Brow, which are semi ancient and natural woodland, eases the eye. Skelwith Fold caravan park hides within the trees and the author commends the owner's efforts for maintaining a balance between the needs for affordable accommodation for visitors and the natural landscape.

There is good reason to believe that the route has been deliberately gentrified – the kissing gate and relatively new wall (150 years – well that's modern to a historian!) which the route passes through, but no

STAGE 4

The Roman road.

Summer rising at Skelwith Fold.

way for a cart with stone, or material for gunpowder production at Haverthwaite, that would make its way to Pull Wyke staithes on the mere for its onward journey. The route most definitely had been reduced to a footpath to prevent this, but the right of way had been respected.

Historians will note that Wyke is the Norse for bay. No great surprise there and gives some idea as to how long the spot was usable. It also gives a clue to the silting up; with coppicing holding water back it would appear that the majority of the silting would be caused by

The Roman road continues.

STAGE 4

A shaded way.

Stormy skies over Pull Wyke.

wholesale destruction of forestry, thus releasing water into the becks, creating erosion, caused by a dramatic increase in the demand for timber for shipping and mining. The author suggests that the damage was done in the late 18th century and probably silted up in the late 19th. This would have been just about the time the mortar was drying on Wykefield Cottage, which no doubt was built at its location to take in the view of the mere and the bay, when any industrial or intensive use of the bay had ceased and the genteel dereliction of disuse looked pleasing to the eye.

Another export from Pull Wyke would have been the easy to work rock, "Wenlock", which comes away in nice big slabs with very little effort. This lies in quarries just above the site on the road to the Drunken Duck. There are some significant industrial archaeological features in the area, but these are not in the public domain and are the home to much very special flora and fauna, so are to be left well alone.

The Roman road keeps on the right, close to the beck, but it is not clear and other routes down the grade have been suggested. There are indications of constructed zig-zags and the walker can make their own mind up as how it descends.

For sometime the author considered that the Roman road crossed above Skelwith Force on an approximate line with the Skelwith Bridge Hotel, which could be standing on the road's foundation. The

STAGE 4

The way down the fell at Pull Wyke.

reasoning for this was the fact this road has to accommodate, along its entire length, the geography it passes through – no great straight road. This one has no choice but to accommodate nature wherever possible. A gentle stream in summer can become a raging torrent in minutes in the winter. The hypothesised route then joined the A593 and all looked reasonably hunky dory except for the fact

STAGE 4

The lost harbour at Pull Wyke.

the lake height, based on the position of Ambleside fort, suggested that parts of this route would be likely to be underwater for much of its length, especially during the wet season.

However, the author might allow himself the chance of hedging his bets, and would suggest this maybe is a Roman a route, not dissimilar to that in Eskdale which would be available at certain times of year and only in certain conditions (it may even explain the ford at Skelwith Bridge; effectively if that was fordable the rest of the route would be passable with care), but there would also be a primary route available at all times and that is the one via Skelwith Fold.

The views are delightful on the way down and the problem of which is the Roman one becomes hypothetical, the view is the thing.

A couple of bloomery sites for the production of iron have been found next to the beck and there is a stark contrast in the colour of the soils, with plenty of charcoal still making its mark.

The exit to the long, descending pasture is clearly marked, and the speed of descent has increased with the ankles taking the strain; mind out for the stray Boy Scouts (Pull Wyke is a favourite area for Scout camps) and the odd sheep tending to the verdant green.

All too soon the B5286 is reached and the twist in the route now becomes apparent.

Wykefield Cottage:
Please keep to the permitted way. There are two private houses where the footpath meets the road. Please respect their privacy.

STAGE 4

Beware the road as the walker needs to cross to the protected footpath. The view toward the mere is the key; it is a damp one and there is a clear edge to Windermere's earlier extent. The road has been heading straight for Pull Wyke, which is the quickest way to Ambleside fort a very short distance away by boat. The Romans were exceptionally good at building craft suitable for such a journey; examples of very large flat bottomed craft have been found on the Rhine allowing for large troop movements in relative comfort over short distances.

Unfortunately the opportunity for the walker is not to be a boat ride. Reeds and mud now fill the bay, where the odd heron wanders along pondering when the next frog will pass. The walker will now note the features of this old inlet and the way it lends itself to being useful to craft, a settlement right on the water's edge to manage it is a certainty and there are building bases above the clearly defined beach.

Note that many of these features are not on a right of way. Please view from the public footpath, which provides a good prospect.

There are also signs of a significantly sized ancient settlement overlooking the bay, but details cannot be published here for want of protection for the site. There are some key elements of sound landscape archaeology around this spot and by now in the adventure the walker can put their observation skills to good use; it's just a case of knowing what to look for.

The author has ruminated as he is wont to do (usually over a good ale) and considers that the walker might be minded to be feeling a trifle miffed at this point. The walker has puffed and panted (well the author did and he has no reason to believe others would not) from Ravenglass to Pull Wyke, kept to the Roman way wherever permissible and then within near spitting distance, the last part of the Roman route is denied. Do not be dismayed. Whilst the direct route is not available the service road will allow for a successful terminus.

The author has already mentioned the issue of shoreline access to Windermere and the newly rich in the late 18 to 19th century buying land with views over the water. The trend is not a new one. The Romans would have enjoyed the view no less. Just as the great houses around the mere required servicing and good access, the Roman villas and industry would require the same. There is no doubt that the mere itself was the main highway, but the need to gather timber, iron ore, livestock and produce would all require roads to connect with the shore and a network of tracks and minor roads would abound. The important factor is ever-present industry – use of the environment, exploitation of its riches, and geological ones abound, combined with a means of extraction. And if there is money to be made there will always be someone willing to make a few denarii; even with a slave workforce food and basic shelter is required, an administration to keep them in order and trades and services to keep the process viable.

The Roman landscape would be heavy with wood smoke, from the vicus at Ambleside, the bath house and villas, plus the charcoal burners, bloomeries and quarries. Hear the sounds of trade in the marketplaces; the barked orders from the fort; the stomp of marching feet; impatient horses waiting for the off scraping the cobbles; the far-off sound of timber being felled and curses spent from quarry workers. The urine putrid stench of the leatherworks, the odd dead dog floating by on a bed of excrement, the drainage system emptying straight into the mere; that is the reality of the past, multi-dimensional. All the bits we want to ignore but are ultimately as important as the bits we want to see – sound and smell – are only in recent times being considered when we think of the past.

Ancient local families had always vied with each other over timber and mineral rights, but with the industrial revolution the ownership of land changed to the newly rich industrialists. Sites with the best views, of what the locals would have seen as nothing more than a 'wet highway', meant that many ancient tracks vanished behind walls, boundaries shifted and much of the indigenous industry around the mere began to decline, coppicing became parkland and imported tree varieties were planted to create landscapes and hide the scars of industry from the eye. The view of today is a result of a lurid attempt to prettify towards an ideal landscape, which is contrary to the archaeology of the place.

There are attempts to make the Lake District National Park a World Heritage site, partly based on the view and the culture. There is a fundamental flaw in the argument. The landscape, earth, rock and tree has lost its physical importance – it has become a conception in the mind – a literary 'misconception' of the actuality of the dynamics of a working landscape. What looked pretty and quaint in the 18th and 19th centuries was hard graft for those living in it; the activities were part of a natural machine, evolution continuing as it should, responding to the supply and demand. The imposed desire of intellectually subversive elites to preserve and tinker with the actual, by imposing a false premise and dictate of heritage landscape and culture, has suffocated the Lake District's natural industrial and agricultural life.

The author's rant over, the walker will want to get along. There is no alternative today but to turn left on to the present road and venture up through Pull Garth Wood towards Brathay. The good news is that you can walk off the road in safety and ease. The footpath crosses over, so do mind for the traffic which can be heavy on the B road. Much of the shoreline around Windermere is in private hands, houses built by rich industrialists getting away from the smoke of their workers' labours from the 18th century onwards. This was a relatively practical way of protecting the mere edge from over-exploitation during the past couple

STAGE 4

Tall barn, Brathay Bridge. Note cornerstone.

of centuries. Now the Lake District is under control of a National Park, the shoreline of all the lakes should be made accessible (with allowance for privacy, adequate protection of stock and care of the natural environment) to all. This undoubtedly will make the author unpopular with a few landowners but no doubt quite popular with fellow walkers. It's about time access rights to a complete circular shoreline walk of Windermere was put in hand, but not Windermere alone.

The author acknowledges that this is maybe, just possibly, another rant. If this is the case he humbly apologises for such a lapse.

Having traversed the wood, which can be a place of wonder when the early spring light glints through the branches and a dark mysterious spot when dark autumn showers trickle down in cascades making the walker wish for the exposure of the open pasture before Brathay, even if it means more of a soaking. The sunlight glints well through the trees, but the roar of traffic can and does intrude in equal measure. The path can be rough in places. For those walkers finding it too much there is a bus stop for Ambleside at the entrance to Skelwith Fold caravan site.

Even with the protection of the path, beware the road as it changes sides on occasions and the road is busy.

Brathay Hall lies over to the right, a grand house looking out over the mere, now a training centre which by its own efforts has become...

...."a leading centre in experiential learning within the commercial industry's ever-changing markets where they apply extraordinary know-how to inspire deep and lasting personal change across a complete range of people from youth to boardroom."

The author considers this to be interesting stuff and can think of no more pleasant a setting for it. Much care has been taken to care for its

STAGE 4

environs as no doubt it is part of the process of understanding – landscapes do have an emotional effect upon us all. Early humankind understood their place in the order of things by creating memorials out of the physical matter, earth and stone and copied the landscape within their henges. A rare find of a Bronze Age axe (found in 2008) suggests that the area was being cleared and cultivated long before the Romans turned up. To the left and peering out from a cluster of trees is Holy Trinity church, reached by the left hand track which would have been the servants' way across the pasture from the Hall, easy to follow if not wet; if so, then a little further along the road and take the left hand turn into the lane.

Sitting on the only bit of rock available to take in this Italianate church, which to the author's mind is no more than a social statement inflicted on the landscape in 1836. It is impossible to miss it unless there is a severe fog or the walker is walking in the dark. To the author there is an element of oddity rather than folly.

No doubt the parishioners disagree and the walker should visit and assist by making a donation to its enormous upkeep. Just because the author does not find it to his liking does not mean that he is correct.

Go and see and make your own mind up! But don't forget a donation.

STAGE 4

The hand of time.

The author does find it interesting that the Redmayne family, who lived at Brathay Hall, could afford such a building from their vast Italian silk importing business, but were not willing to have it in their immediate confines. But there may have been a purpose in that. Curiously it faces north-south because it wouldn't fit on the natural stone base if east to west; the clue to the problem of orientation is the name of the lane, Bog Lane. So not only did the Redmaynes not want the church too close to Brathay Hall, but also built it on the cheapest bit of land possible and on the wrong orientation. But no doubt it looked good, "we have arrived, we have travelled, we are cultured and can afford the latest European style", this being the undoubted message, singing out loud and clear, to passers-by on the road to Ambleside. The church, along with its associated buildings, sits within trees which are a little later, though there are some that could be as old as its construction, suggesting somebody tried to hide it quite quickly. For the most part they have succeeded. Well done them!

A very narrow footbridge, subsequently widened, was erected to allow people to get away from this fine edifice as quickly as possible. The bridge is a marvellous piece of work and has survived everything the river Brathay can throw at it. This bridge puts the walker on the main road, which alas is not a place to be for any length of time. You could avoid this prospect by walking back from the church to the junction, turn left, and proceed to Brathay Bridge – the scene of one of the author's more spectacular pieces of personal research.

The approach to Brathay Bridge is usually obscured by a huddle of motor cars, but it is clear that much has been done to manage the flow of the river. The walker will have noted that the road has kept to a high bit of ground, looking down a little towards the church, but the author has a suspicion that the Roman road lies in the grounds of Brathay Hall to the right and approaches the present bridge site through Brathay Farm, which has some splendid buildings rather too close to the river without substantial foundations, which makes the author suspect a bigger bridge.

Brathay bridge was certainly in place in 1643 when it is mentioned in respect of Parliamentary forces stationed in the area; it is much earlier than the English Civil War; there are clear signs of rebuilding, perhaps three bits of widening, although the records show only two. The author is wondering if the bridge was part of an earlier one, that is to say the base of the cutwaters between the two arches potentially sitting on Roman bridge remains, surmising that the

You have been warned!

Brathay footbridge, twice its original width.

STAGE 4

Dappled shades of sunlight at Brathay footbridge. A truly magnificent piece of engineering, providing access to the church.

pontus was much larger than the present having to accommodate a longer crossing than present.

To establish this hypothesis close examination of the base of the bridge was required. The author is not known for his agility, other than to get to the nearest place of refreshment, but managed by cautious means to get out to the centre of the bridge, choosing a dry patch in the season to do so. Even so this is not to be recommended, nor should be wandering into a river prone to spate be on a list of things to do, just for the fun of it.

Archaeology is a fascination. The author admits that when he is on the trail of something he can be somewhat 'detached', so he was taking no notice of the activities above until the dribble of warm liquid started running down his neck. And it came as an equal shock to the individual on the bridge top to hear a voice seemingly coming from nowhere that it would be appreciated if he didn't chuck his coffee off the bridge. The author considers it could have been worse.

The answer as to the bridge's age is that it is a considerable one and unlike the rough finish of the present bridge there are indications of much earlier and more refined work beneath. As to the fact this bridge could have been longer is still open to debate. The author thinks it was of more prominence on the Brathay Farm side. The present arch arrangement is undoubtedly to ease the flow. There are some very impressive buildings close-by – large barns exceptionally tall – with re-used stone incorporated into their walls.

The walker, having already met with water as being the fastest route, could consider no bridge at Brathay Farm and a very quick punt ride to the fort. The author does not disagree, but the flow of the Brathay could well be of use and the structure could have incorporated a watermill. This would enhance the reason for a bridge's construction, the premise being that there is a high population, the troops and vicus and a workforce, plus a desire to keep grain and flour dry. There is clear evidence of a mill pond and weir above the bridge, raising the level of the river and holding it back. The river has not managed to obliterate its past bondage. The mill pond is in fact the best evidence that the present road course is a modern one as it is built over part of the original pond. Thus the road must have gone via the grounds of the hall.

Note: There is no pavement for this crossing and traffic levels are high. TAKE EXTREME CARE investigating the bridge.

Brathay church rooms.

A fashion icon.

Brathay church.

STAGE 4

A secluded moment in Brathay.

Walkers should also note this area is called Clappersgate, the meaning of which seems to be "stones for a bridge by a road", which seems reasonably appropriate.

The walker will note the very steep grade out of the Brathay to the main road. There is no escape from the main road; turn right and proceed towards Ambleside. Beware all the way as this is a particularly nasty journey, but a short one. There is a wide footpath that the odd cyclist will use, but it is a noisy environment and is best shook off as quickly as possible.

Loughrigg Fell lies across the way and there are excursions that prevent much of this walk along the road. Consult your ordnance survey map as to which the walker may prefer, but watch the time, especially in autumn and remember how far has already been traversed before attempting.

If staying on the A593, as the walker approaches the pinch point of roads crossing the Rothay, use the attractive little footbridge on the right. Once across you are in the Roman vicus and somewhere under the boot is the Roman road heading towards Keswick.

Depending on the time of day and personal condition after a day of adventure, the walker may decide not to head for Ambleside fort until tomorrow. The fort is worthy of a second glance, even if at the first it seems less than inspiring. The walker by this stage will know better than to take things at first glance. The author suggests heading into town to one of the many comfortable places for refreshment. A full list of venues, from Hotels to B&Bs, will make for a cosy night.

Ambleside, having a plentiful supply of water cascading through it, took full advantage of the free energy and with favourable conditions and a plentiful wood supply. It became a centre for bobbin manufacture, supplying the cotton mills of Lancashire. The arrival of the railway at Windermere, and subsequently Lakeside, opened up the mere and the magnificent environs to the many, much to the annoyance of the newly rich who had seen the Lakes as theirs; and prevented much access and new construction near the banks – "not on my front lawn". Ambleside, being a commercial centre with plenty of pubs for the bobbin mill workers, saw an opportunity to profit from these restrictions and swiftly responded. With connections to Keswick, and magnificent scenery between the two it flourished and still does. Ambleside is a living, thriving community, not merely a tourist destination bereft of life when the tourists depart, and the author commends the efforts of local people of keeping it so.

However there is a hidden past to the place. Let us delve back in time a little.

September 15, 1437, Grant, for life, to William Clement, groom of the chamber, of the office of master forester of the forest of Troutebek and Ambilsede in the lordship of Kendale, to hold himself or by deputy, with the accustomed wages etc.; Cal. Pat. R. 1437, p. 92.
Farrer W & Curwen J.F (eds.) "Records relating to the Barony of Kendale": volume 2, Institute of Historical Research, (1924)

STAGE 4

The previous text provides a very useful insight into the history of Ambleside. If nothing else it confirms that by 1437 the forest is a well controlled, established administration, managed in a very professional manner to provide income for landowners and a workforce accordingly. The routine of identifying which trees could be felled for which purpose, what stock could be kept in the forests and how the land should be harvested for its multi-various purposes all fell within his domain – no small job, requiring considerable knowledge and experience. William was in control of the lands latterly of the Earl of Kendal, or to be precise lands controlled by the late Duke of Bedford, John of Lancaster, who had died in 1435; the title of Earl of Kendal was not to re-emerge till 1443 when it was added to the titles of the Earl of Somerset. To some eyes this could be viewed as a dry document without much further depth, but there is much more beneath. One has to look outside the Lakes to find it.

1437 sees the period of the English Regency coming to an end; Henry VI is already crowned King of France, a culmination of English 'control' of France (but in fact a turning point against English rule), is now old enough to claim the English throne. The English economy is stable enough to afford a long standing war to claim France.

More locally, back in the Lake Counties timber supplies are important to the running of the army and navy, bark is required for tanning, iron cannot be made without charcoal and all manner of commodities are needed to maintain a war effort and a healthy economy. Thus forests such as Troutbeck and Ambleside are part of a long chain of production that keeps the War economy afloat.

However, it is another commodity, more to do with the wider aspects of trade in fine goods and thus the nation's cash wealth that is suddenly at stake. Wool.

Two years earlier in 1435 the hard pressed, but certainly not bowed, King Charles VII of France bribed the Duke of Burgundy, leader of the Flemish speaking states (allied to the English), to break his allegiance, by means of economic warfare, thus damaging an incredibly important part of the English economy – the wool trade. Export of wool to the Flemish states in Europe came to a halt and tax revenues collapsed. Every alternative to keep the economy and thus the war effort afloat was to be considered fast as the Spanish were taking advantage of the open marketplace. The great English danger was that exports of wool from Spain would sideline English wool for good. Such a collapse in the wool trade would have a significant effect within the Lake Counties. To this day the town of Kendal has "Wool is my bread" as its motto. Take the trade in one commodity out of the mix and the whole suffers. A practical means of levering a change of heart by the Duke of Burgundy could be employed and one which the area of Ambleside and Troutbeck could be well employed to do: Gunpowder production.

Gunpowder had been in production in Britain since the thirteenth century. Now it may come as a surprise to some that Ambleside and district would have been fully aware of the use of black powder for mining. Warfare is a way of promoting and exploiting new technologies – a means of destroying castle walls by either blasting a hole in them, or by use of a few barrels of powder strategically placed beneath their walls, is always going to be more practical than siege engines. Getting the barrels there requires miners. If you want the job done efficiently, every baron, lord and earl in every county in England had to provide

Reflections near Ambleside.

the King with skilled personnel towards the war effort. The chances are that those surviving the experience bring back some knowledge of the wider world. Witnessing the practical demonstration of the effect of gunpowder offers opportunity for all concerned to benefit from it. A means of acquiring the knowledge to replicate would be advantageous, so it comes as no surprise that there are very scant records of the recipe and detailed methods. The control of knowledge makes individuals powerful.

The experts at 'black powder' were the Germans, notably the Nürnburg school of powder makers, in Bavaria. These highly skilled individuals travelled across Europe fully aware of the political complications of each state, but as contractors they seem to have been able to keep their skills to themselves; they were chemists and geologists long before the terms were recognised. These roving experts are 'individuals', not corporations, nor should they be confused by the later Elizabethan intervention of Germans employed by the Crown at Keswick. We are looking at personages prized by nobility and royalty for their specific skills. Where illustrations exist of the firing of cannon the 'firemaster' and the cannon is often as not centre stage, in good detail. These were individuals that played for extremely high stakes in an already dangerous world and benefited from patronage for their efforts.

Now the question arises – did they bring the powder with them, or did they make it on the spot?

The transportation of gunpowder would be readily understood, there being a war on, with ever increasing use of the material, so it is possible that incredibly dangerous and expensive powder was brought into the country explicitly for the equally important extraction of precious minerals, such as copper. Only the nobility or the Crown could afford such expenditure. However, because of the complications of delivering ample supplies over many years to various mining projects, it seems equally likely that Ambleside and Troutbeck provided the Germans with all the ingredients they needed and the production process was readily understood, so long distance costly transportation is unlikely. However well the Germans tried, the locals could not be kept out of the production loop and a home-grown set of experts would begin to emerge. The same thing had happened in Italy back in the 1360s, resulting in the Italians better understanding the potential of gunpowder.

Another clue to the impact of this northerly but most important bit of England is who was the major landlord, in this case the Earl of Kendal until 1365, better known as the 1st Duke of Bedford, third surviving son of King Henry IV, married to the Duke of Burgundy's daughter until she died in 1432. 1365 is, of course, the year the French persuade the Duke of Burgundy to change sides; the influence of John's previous marriage having passed, he antagonised the Burgundians by marrying Jacquetta of Luxembourg with direct links to the Holy Roman Empire, thus giving England an alliance more powerful than the Dukes of Burgundy found comfortable.

So one of William Clement's tasks was, no doubt, to provide adequate coppice for charcoal production – not for iron making, but for the gunpowder industry. He would have been readily aware of the vital importance of a burgeoning new product and the effect it would have.

But more importantly he would know the location of potassium nitrate and sulphur, the two most sought-after ingredients in Europe for gunpowder manufacture. Externally, Iceland was the biggest exporter of sulphur, because they had the volcanoes providing a copious supply. The Italians were not far behind. Potassium nitrate can be made from wood ash and quick lime – no shortage of that locally, but Sulphur? That is a hard nut to crack, unless you understand the qualities of iron pyrites, which produces sulphur, and there's no shortage of that. Bingo and heyho, all the ingredients in one spot and no having to send to Iceland for a bag or two!

Have we any evidence of this early production of gunpowder in the area?

Possibly.

Throughout the Lakes, especially on managed bracken lands, there are sites used for converting green bracken and birch twigs into nitrate of potash. These are often associated with soap manufacture, or fertilizers. It may be that they had a much wider use, potentially in early gunpowder manufacture. The number of these sites seems significant.

We also have much evidence of the potentials for the industry, notably the known practical demonstration (warfare) of the usefulness of the material that assists in extracting precious minerals. We have experts wandering all over Europe and all the ingredients to do it made available to them, and a reason for doing it. Increase in extraction of mineral wealth made up for a shortfall caused by the wool industry being in flux and a need to build up the country's arsenal.

This is a classic case of us experts needing to do more research and what started off as a quick discourse for the reader on the history of Ambleside leads to some serious archaeological research – that's the fun thing about archaeology. It grows on you.

Silence where man's foot trod near Ambleside.

In Cumbria the inclement weather caused problems for millers – you can't mill damp corn. The answer was a drying bed to get any dampness out. These drying beds were also ideal for the gunpowder industry along with the milling machinery. The opportunity for converting from corn to milling gunpoweder cake with a good profit potential (if you survived) would be tempting. The technical term for this gunpowder process is "corning". Whether this relates initially to the use of the building rather than the process is open to debate – but it is one explanation.

There was an increase in the mining of copper during this period, which inevitably was enhanced by the use of explosives feeding a war effort with a need to find ways round a massive hole in the country's finances; powder production to kill the enemy doesn't just mean putting it in cannons, but in increasing metal production.

An increase in the English gunpowder industry would eventually filter back to foreign ears. The Duke of Burgundy relaxed the importation dues for wool, breaking with the French, mostly because of the disruption in trade which, whilst initially beneficial to him, ultimately destabilised the market and began to bite back. The Duke's family was very interested in arms manufacture, especially guns, and the Duke's father and forefather had invested heavily in the technology – he would understand the significance of the potential threat. The Duke was married to Margaret of Bavaria – there may be a link to gunpowder and armaments here! The English were renowned for iron manufacture and casting.

With German gunpowder expertise the effect could be painful. This is no exaggeration of the effectiveness of even small scale production – iron quality and gunpowder were subjects discussed at the highest level of state, much as this generation discusses inter-continental ballistic missiles where the very threat of them has in fact more impact than the real thing. Combine iron manufacture and gunpowder and you have more effective cannon – base both in a virtually inexhaustible supply of natural material for same and you have a winning mix. Display the same to an authoritative audience and that audience takes note.

Careful balancing of the desire for weaponry and the powder to make them work would prove vital in a diplomatic as well as a practical sense and the initial success of the early works in the Lake Counties dwindles correspondingly to the change in the direction of the Duke of Burgundy. There is reason to believe that once the crisis had passed and the technology was well understood by a wider audience that production dwindled in the north – a small amount merely for specialist local use.

Strangely, within three years of Clement's appointment he is retired on a full pension. Perhaps, as the crisis had passed the need for Clements to manage the forests in a particular way was no longer required. It does seem somewhat odd, considering the timescale required to make change in the landscape, how short this tenure is – unless of course Clement was in fact more than just a forestry manager?

Production of gunpowder headed south, closer to the capital and the naval bases, and the easiest way to gain extra supplies was to steal it off the French. The author believes that the availability of all the ingredients meant that the industry never went away. An interesting factor in the opening of the first industrial scale mill at Sedgewick by John Wakefield in the 1770s in a very public place seems not to cause the slightest alarm. It is possible that the locals are in fact quite un-phased by such works because they are quite at ease with them. Dangerous activities they may be, but profitable. There is reason to consider that there was an inherent understanding of the material. The echoes of the very early production continued down through the years and in use within mines when required throughout that time. This later renewal of production relied heavily on international imports – easy when you control the globe.

So William Clement's appointment and subsequent early retirement opens up yet another enquiry into the importance of Cumbria and the people within it. There are so many other adventures that take us from the local to the international within the landscape and you don't have to dig deep to find them. Have a go, you will be amazed.

As part of the forward-thinking of the populous, a major refurbishment of Ambleside is underway making it a fit and proper example of generous care and attention to detail and service that Cumbria is rightly proud of. The modern Ambleside is further away from the mere than the Roman equivalent; this is probably more to do with the power source for running the bobbin mills – the becks that run off the fell to join the river Rothay could be easily harnessed.

The footbridge over the Rothay is modern but blends in well; it has a 'seasoned' feel and reflects the Rothay. Realising it is now free of encroaching Ambleside, through stone built banks and culverts, it now enjoys a natural edge on its way to the mere. A settled scene, spoiled only by the noise of the traffic and echoed only by the sound of the winter torrents that sometimes submerge the bridge.

The walker should follow the path that brings them to the sports ground, under which lies part of the Roman vicus, the civilian settlement. This now sub-surface feature continues right down (and nearly into) the fort and also by the then water's edge; no doubt some of the properties took advantage of this waterside location.

The author muses to think that trade still goes on; the sports ground has a regular Car Boot sale.

The present day walker sees a gentle (at most times) river Rothay chuckling along towards the mere. The Romans would have seen an expanse of water, one which would stretch over to the present A593 at Clappersgate and right up to Rydal Water, as we now know it, not very deep perhaps in places, with water meadow and farming where the present Ambleside lies. But water, nonetheless, would dominate the scene. In brief – put a metre back on Windermere and the scenery changes dramatically.

Beyond the sports ground, on the right, is a very grand barn sitting in a field. The author always gives these barns a good close inspection, because it's amazing how much re-used stone they have in them and the odd inscription or architectural feature from an earlier age turns up. Alas, in this case nothing, but it does look the part. The author has often wondered whether the design of these barns has a little to do with Roman granaries – the roof line, the grand solidity of the structure – perhaps it is just an echo, but vernacular architecture builds on purpose and develops through example. Granaries in Roman forts are substantial structures; at Birdoswald on Hadrian's Wall the southern granary was converted into a hall in the latter days of the Roman occupation and beyond. It is credible to consider that these structures have survived long enough to have an influence on the long barn design in Cumbria.

*   *   *

The author is aware that this has not been a very long distance walk, but it has provided some of the best contact with Roman infrastructure other than Hadrian's Wall, in the country. The fact that the walker can march along a Roman road between two forts through magnificent passes and also add to the knowledge base is significant. It provides some indication of how little we know.

There is still much to be done in respect of understanding the route, its usefulness and its administration. We have most of the bones, very little of the muscle and none of the flesh.

STAGE 4

Stage Five

Ambleside (Galava)

Galava

In 1913 the Archaeologist, historian, and philosopher R.G. Collingwood set to work on the excavation of Galava, lying beneath Borrans Field in Ambleside, as the result of pottery being found in area in 1875, in what subsequently has been identified as the fort vicus. *This area is now under the Rugby club grounds and includes a well-constructed road and a series of buildings.*

Owing to unforeseen circumstances caused by World War 1 the excavation halted in 1915 and only recommenced in 1920. Collingwood was, as every good archaeologist should be, an observer and his analysis was excellent. The walker will note that Collingwood fitted Galava in amidst many other significant excavations in Cumbria over a relatively short period of time as his other academic interests kept him equally absorbed. However, the excavation was well advanced in 1914 and Collingwood was able to report that there was evidence of an early fort, with its slightly unusual off-square design which seemed to date from a pre Hadrianic period, with the emphasis, or impetus, on the part of the Roman Army to make itself secure rather than to build to an otherwise normal set design (square or card shaped). The coin evidence offered a starting point for the date of the forts, with examples from the reigns of Augustus and Claudius being represented.

To the author this would suggest an early military establishment in the area during the campaigns of Petilius Cerialis as governor in AD71 (possibly using a 'camp' nearer the vicus rather than the present fort site), followed by the equally significant adventures of Gnaeus Julius Agricola AD 76 to 82/3. Collingwood opted for Agricola as the builder of the fort and this seems a firm foundation date for the main site.

A coin from the reign of Hadrian points to a rebuilding of the fort on a more standard perimeter layout providing a continuity of Roman military presence and purpose. Collingwood opted for abandonment after the Agricolan period rather than continuity, but the ceramic ware found on the site seems to bridge the gap between Agricola and Hadrian, suggesting a constant if not military use of the site. Coins from later in the Roman Empire of Julia Domna (170-217), wife of the Roman Emperor Lucius Septimius Severus and Valens (AD378), suggest a continuous use of the site.

The early fort construction is thus described: *"Whose rampart, of puddled clay, on a cobble foundation"*, with a double ditch on the outside with an overall site appearance, as ever accurately described by Collingwood as *"an irregular quadrilateral"*, it seems to have some

STAGE 5

sophistication for an otherwise relatively temporary (by nature of its wooden construction) structure, because Collingwood identified guardrooms by the gates with glazing in the windows. By 1941, the granary was excavated and it is in the true and honourable tradition of archaeology that Collingwood continued his quest whilst the world around him was physically falling apart in the catastrophe of yet another World War. Archaeologists rise above such things. We serve a higher purpose.

Perhaps most significantly, since Collingwood's excavations, the remains of a dock facility on the lake edge have been discovered, clearly identifying how the lake played a significant role in goods transportation.

The name of *Galava* does not come from an inscription from the site but from the "Antonine Itinerary", effectively a Roman AA map, identifying journeys and sites throughout Britain. In this instance it is the "iter X" in which the site is listed as being 18 miles from GLANNOVENTA Ravenglass and 12 miles from ALAVANA Watercrook.

The author will offer the walker one piece of sound research advice – matching actual forts to the "Antonine Itinerary" is a lifetime's work, especially when an archaeologist comes up with another fort site! This sort of thing does tend to put a spoke in the academic works, somewhat. The major problem is the lack of fort name inscriptions, such as dedications to the rebuilding of granaries and forts themselves. Such inscription slabs are handy building materials and in the most part vanished with the collapse of the Roman world in the west.

The walker has the benefit of some interpretation boards and the outline of the later fort is presented in a rural way. Cattle roam the area and the fencing around the restored building outlines is heavy – the foundations are gradually disappearing beneath the sod. But the walker should not be disturbed. The National Trust has volunteers that can easily tidy the place up. The keen eyed will notice the landscape reveals much of the past without the need for notices and stonework. The shoreline change, where Windermere once lapped on two sides of the fort, is now land; the land towards Keswick, outside the fort which housed the vicus which stretched on for someway towards modern Ambleside, straddles the then Roman road. The traces of the irregularity of the earlier fort and the use of some of the local geology for parts of the vicus – all are there for the walker to explore.

Amazing what you can see if you observe.

However, genteel and sylvan landscapes aside, the author considers that the obvious original need for a secure point seems a tad undermined by the location. The walker will note that there is deal of 'up' around the fort. Admittedly the immediate environs are flat, suggesting that before the fort was constructed somebody might well have been taking advantage of the area for trade and administration, because the land would hardly be usable for crops, being rather too close to the mere and its inlets. The fort's immediate location would have seen water on two sides and possibly a third, leaving only the side facing Keswick as a dry approach. It is effectively a peninsula of silt and reeds, sitting on a rock base, that pokes through the otherwise flat plain as a none-too-subtle reminder as to what allows them to consider stopping on the spot.

How could such an exposed location be suitable for a Roman fort?

The campaigns of Petilius Cerialis, in particular, were significant in more ways than one. In military terms Cerialis undertakes several apparently suicidal campaigns from York, through hostile territory. The occupation of Carlisle, requiring traversing lands of the Brigante and the sub tribes of the region (including the Carvetii) is of considerable note. This would require a march over some extremely demanding landmass with plenty of opportunity for the tribes to attack his forces. However, Cerialis seems to have benefited from a civil war within the Brigante, one of which the sub tribes seem to have taken advantage of, by keeping out of it.

How can the author make such a hypothesis?

Because of the remarkably exposed location of the Roman sites at Ambleside. Watercrook (Kendal) and Carlisle, to name but a few.

Now the historians amongst you will no doubt check the Roman occupation dates for these sites, especially Ambleside. More work needs to be undertaken at all the sites and the author offers Ravenglass as an example. The earliest fort site had another beneath it, only seen on the last day of the dig and never fully recorded, and no samples of the wooden structure survived for analysis, because the techniques were in their infancy. Thus the record shows early Hadrianic, but the testimony of those present states earlier and the pottery washed out of the fort on every tide suggests likewise. The earliest excavations at Ambleside require close scrutiny in respect of pottery from the earlier fort site, as evidenced by the re-interpretation of dates for Roman pottery at Chelmsford, where the dates go significantly backwards from that previously considered and pottery is an excellent material to associate with places, trade and dates.

You see, we archaeologists don't know everything! There is room for interpretation and discovery even with the material we think we know. Why not get involved and discover for yourselves?

It is one thing to invade a territory, but a completely different one to stay happily in it. The fortifications will provide relief, but the supply lines to the fort are the weak link. There is little doubt that the locals were quite willing to supply goods and services – the existing administration of the tribal system was already in decline having been eroded long before Claudius decided to formally open up Britannia for business. This was no different in the north; opposition was met, as the Roman formal occupation drove north, but the corrosive policy of 'civilisation' referred to by Tacitus (actually a reference to Roman moral purpose and the quality of Romans in a translucent veiled attack on the psychotic Emperor Domitian) did most of the work ahead of the need for the sword. When Britons eventually realised that the policy of co-operation, imposed by their leaders, actually meant 'enslavement' (Tacitus again) it was too late. The Romanisation had become too strong and the whole had split into factions most easily swayed by the need to respond to the new economics of being part of an Empire. In other words...

...the Roman military command could monitor intelligence and respond to tribal activity over large swathes of northern Britannia because of good military intelligence, provided by traders operating in the territories.

A Roman grave marker found at Ambleside has created a potential counter argument about the relationship between the locals and the Roman army.

D B M FLA ROMANVS ACT VIXIT ANNI XXXV IN CAS INTE AB HOSTI

Roman road heading for Keswick via the Vicus at Ambleside.

"To the good spirits of the departed Flavius Romanus, actarius, he lived for thirty-five years, [killed] in service whilst standing up to the enemy." (RIB 755.a; secondary)

Alternatively, as this was found in the fort area it is unlikely to be in its original setting as burial of bodies, or cremation, was forbidden within fort or settlements. This would include the immediate environs, including the vicus. The author considers it unlikely that a grave marker would be robbed out for building material – it would be seen as 'bad form' and unlucky. The author has a suspicion that this particular grave marker is a 'jibe' at an imperial military scribe. The actual grave marker is inscribed roughly and the author would suggest, with some venom, no attempt at art. Somebody was putting the proverbial boot in on an individual that spent more of his time scribbling on clay tablets rather than marching to Hardknott and back. Such comfortable jobs would understandably cause offence in the ranks.

The inscription now lies in Tullie House museum, Carlisle.

This is in contrast to the other marker from Ambleside which suggests a good life.

D B M FLA FVSCINVS EME EX ORDI VISI AN LV

STAGE 5

Signs of Vicus structure with stone back wall shelf.

Ambleside fort: not looking its best!

"To the good spirits of the departed and Flavius Fuscinus, veteran, former ordinarius, he lived for fifty-five years." (RIB 755.a; primary)

Fifty five is a good age and a man who has spent his adult life in the army, retired, no doubt farming or trading and living on his pension, probably living in the vicus, or nearby, and keeping in touch with the

STAGE 5

Signs of Vicus structures incorporating stone back wall shelf.

The ancient water's edge t Ambleside, with indication of mooring fixings.

life of the army by drinking with the troops in the bars. The term *ordinarius* suggests a senior military individual and is obviously identified as an honour, the senior rank reached by Fuscinus.

The author will have noticed that the inscriber of most Roman monuments use abbreviations. It saves on space and is easier on the chisel!

Why this marker was found within the vicinity of the fort is a mystery, but a mystery is there to be solved. Have a go. We archaeologists do not have all the answers! Special areas were set aside for cremations and burials with clearly delineated boundaries. Military personnel liked to be buried alongside main roads so that they would not be forgotten by

Ambleside Fort – a less than impressive presentation.

Taking it easy before the next tourists arrive.

their fellow soldiers, and through the seeing of the grave markers the memory of the departed lived on in the present. Gone but not forgotten.

The general condition of the exposed fort remains, and while reasonably well interpreted with information boards are, at the time of the author writing (2008), in need of a very good weed. The occasional cow pancake cannot be avoided, so do mind where you stand.

Getting underway at Ambleside.

Let's go for a trip.

But the walker should not be dismayed as there is plenty to see in this parkland, which is not enclosed within stout cattle-proof fencing.

The cows should be treated with respect. Do not annoy them as they are easily annoyed, especially if they have young which they naturally will wish to protect. If they have decided to use the fence protecting the restored remains as a scratching post, pass by and return when they have finished. There is no hurry.

NEVER run away from a cow. If a cow decides to approach you with an enthusiastic intent, no doubt just to say 'hello', but the speed of that enthusiasm worries, just raise an arm and give a good hearty yell. Continue to flap arms and walk towards the cow. The reaction is usually one of astonishment and a cessation of the desire of a closer and immediate need to say 'how do you do'. NEVER EVER RUN!

The walker, free from bovine curiosity, will be able to walk where boats were once moored on the beach and the earlier fort outline is reasonably clear, taking advantage of the natural rock features. The vicus lies towards the Keswick end of the site, in fact in the next two fields straddling the Roman road heading that way – now a wonderful hay meadow and a sports ground. Note that the vicus is away from the business end of the site, where the fort has a good view of the

MV Swan at Ambleside.

Early morning on the mere. No crowds and bustle; just the smell of bacon and the prospect of a day's sailing ahead – bliss.

Gone aground at Watersedge.

mere. Boats can moor and be offloaded, trade can be observed and taxed, but nothing is allowed to obscure the view. Practical advantages from a military point of view would be to keep a clear killing zone, somewhat unlikely, but part of a military regime. More likely it's a case of keeping a distance from a mere that can dramatically vary in water level.

Windermere, so named after a Norse individual by the name of Winander *(Defoe)*, lies just beyond the reed bed. The Brathay and Rothay join by the fort and there is an enjoyable walk on what was water, until the silts built up, out to the mere's edge. There is absolutely no doubt that the Romans inherited an established waterway system here, and merely developed it to their advantage and need. Archaeologically, the mere has

An Ambleside morning.

given up few of its earliest secrets. The most significant factor is the depth of the mere. The present level is the result of water being pumped out for United Utilities to leak all over the place (but at least it makes it back into the mere – eventually) and the dredging near Fell Foot on the way to the Swan at Newby Bridge, where the first steam passenger pleasure boats were based. This dredging, to allow the pleasure launches to pass, created a dramatic change in the mere level. The author has studied the

Ambleside delight.

Off the wall!

landscape around Newby Bridge and concludes a vast area of mere, although already shallow and reed strewn by the beginning of the nineteenth century, dried up as a result of this dredging. An improved egress point allowed more water to head for Haverthwaite and beyond, necessitating a weir to control the flow. Industry was also calling upon the water supply, with iron foundries and chemical processes for the explosives and washing soda. The pleasure trips became so popular that the capacity was exceeded, so Lakeside station was built in deep water so larger vessels could easily come about.

The old roads, now back lanes, still follow the original mere edge.

On a sunny day the site of Galava is a pleasant place and the walker can imagine what a very pleasant posting this could be. When it's raining, the view physically changes dramatically. The clouds huddle in above the site sitting on the water, the drizzle seeps into every crevice and the shine of such a spot wears off. The Romans undoubtedly had villas in the area, but the author would suggest that, even allowing for changes in weather patterns, the mere would have been a very quiet spot in winter. The soldiers on guard duty, facing the

RoyalOak in Ambleside.

mere, must have had good reason to look forward to the end of their shift.

Waterhead, a very short distance away, has a little flavour of the Roman past – jetties and places to eat and drink, a general hubbub, crowds waiting for boats, and others just watching the scene.

The walker must consider Galava to be the terminus of the trip.

The author is aware that the journey has only been 36 kilometres, but it has been a very exhilarating 36.

The tradition of getting the feet wet at the end of the walk is not really to be recommended at Galava. Much better to get the throat wet instead!

You have walked a strategic communications route of the Roman Empire and assisted in bringing an ancient route back into the public view.

Footnote
"Guide to Ravenglass: An Unusual Archaeological Guide" 2009
"The Cockermouth Ring" 2010 (Full guide)
"Ravenglass-Miterdale – Ullock to Cockermouth" 2011 (Full Guide)

Getting Involved in Archaeology

The desire to explore, to grasp the nettle like pleasure of wanting to know why, or just enjoying the sensation of wonder – these things are at the very heart of archaeology.

Archaeology is the opportunity to stand up to your knees in mud in pouring rain and sleet and still have a childlike amazement at everything the earth wants to give up.

With walking, the landscape is ever changing, not just because of passing through it but because it will have changed the moment it has been walked through by the walker; imperceptibly perhaps, but it will have changed. There are millions upon millions of tiny actions, eroding or constructing the scene, with mankind constantly attempting to make an indelible mark. Archaeologists like tracing those footsteps and wondering at their passing.

Wanting to know what yesterday was like is at the heart of archaeology.

Having spent over twenty years studying the Romans on the West Cumbrian coast the author is perhaps now able to change a full stop, on the amount we know, to a comma, perhaps adding a sentence or two. That gives you a sense of scale of the task.

Research suggests Roman affiliated coastal trading was being carried out as a precursor to the campaigns by Petilius Cerealis in AD 71, followed by likely western-coastal-estuary-based temporary camps and forts of Agricola in AD77/8, with Trajanic forts providing a fluid defense renewed and strengthened by Hadrian in AD122 onwards. Hardknott and the road through the passes fall squarely into this era of Roman military expansion.

And that's just for one small bit of the local landscape in Cumbria and only accounts for the early years of Roman influence. There's at least another three hundred years to go!

And that of course is just the Roman part. There are thousands of years of mankind to look at, to study, and to get involved in wherever the walker hails from. This walk offers a Roman bias, but the industrial heritage of Eskdale might inspire the walker just as equally.

And the glorious thing about archaeology is the fact it's not all digging holes; there is a myriad of ways in which anybody can get involved.

So how to get involved where you live?
For starters join the CBA.

Every part of Britain has some story to tell which is woven into our soils, landscapes and buildings. This historic environment is one of our richest resources and gives a special quality to our lives. It is also irreplaceable. Yet, because we live and work in it, it is easily overlooked or squandered. Nothing stays the same. Change made the past, just as it will shape the future. But we owe it to those who follow us to find ways of managing change so that they will have a past for themselves. This is why the CBA exists: to give a voice to Britain's past, and to help enrich the time to come.

The CBA is a network of individuals, national and regional organisations which cover Britain. The CBA welcomes everyone with a concern for our historic environment. By joining us you:

Give us resources to develop our work in education, conservation and providing information. Strengthen the profile of archaeology in the minds of decision-makers. Individual membership also brings:
Six issues of our flagship magazine British Archaeology including CBA Briefing with projects and events in which you can be involved. Three issues of the Members' Newsletter, with news of the latest CBA projects and initiatives. Membership of a CBA Region. A voice in the work of the Council. Our Annual Report.
Find out more at http://www.britarch.ac.uk/

To join the CBA as an individual member send £32.00 by cheque/postal order/money order in sterling to the address given below, or use our secure online shop:
   http://www.britarch.ac.uk/shop/index.html
Joint membership is available for two individuals living at the same address for £38.00. Student membership is £19.00 (proof of accreditation required).
Membership of our Young Archaeologists' Club costs only £12.00. Combined family membership, including membership of the CBA and YAC, is also available for £40.00.

Council for British Archaeology, St Mary's House, 66 Bootham, York YO30 7BZ United Kingdom
Telephone (+44) (0) 1904 671417. Fax (+44) (0) 1904 671384
Email: info@britarch.ac.uk

  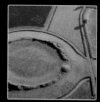

General Information

Transport

National Rail Enquiries
http://www.nationalrail.co.uk/
Tel: 0845 7484950

Ticket Booking
http://www.thetrainline.com

Northern Rail
http://www.northernrail.org/
Barrow-in-Furness to Carlisle
The Cumbrian Coastline (including Ravenglass & Eskdale Railway),
Timetable 6
General Customer Helpline (for comments/complaints/queries)
Tel: 0845 000 0125
Email – Customer Relations
customer.relations@northernrail.org
Telesales & Bookings Tel: 0845 700 0125
Access/Disabled Information & Cycle Assistance
assistance@northernrail.org
Tel: 0845 600 8008
Lost Property
lost.property@northernrail.org
Tel: 0870 602 3322

First Transpennine Express
http://www.tpexpress.co.uk/
Windermere

Virgin Trains
http://www.virgintrains.co.uk/
Euston to Oxenholme the Lake District

Mainline Railway Stations applicable to route
Ravenglass for Eskdale: No Service Sunday
Windermere: Daily

Ravenglass & Eskdale Railway: Daily (limited in winter)
Tel: 01229 717171

Stagecoach North West
http://www.stagecoachbus.com/northwest/index.html
Tel: 01228 597222
Service No's 6, X6 Ravenglass 516

AA Travel
Sunday Service to Ravenglass

Journeyplanner North East & Cumbria
http://www.traveline.info/index.htm
or 0871 200 22 33

Cumbria Tourism
Useful links page
http://www.golakes.co.uk

Taxis

Gosforth Taxis (for Wasdale Link)
Tel. 019467 25308

Ambleside Taxi Service
Tel: 015394 33842

Steves Taxis
Tel: 01539 433544

Grasmere Taxi Services
01539 435506

Kevin's Taxis
01539 432371

John's Taxi
01539 432857

Billy's Taxis
01539 431287

Medical

Hospitals

West Cumberland Hospital
Hensingham, Whitehaven, Cumbria CA28 8JG
Tel: 01946 693181

Westmorland General Hospital
Burton Road, Kendal LA9 7RG
Tel: 01539 732288

Health Centres

Seascale Health Centre
Gosforth Road, Seascale, Cumbria CA20 1PN
Tel: 019467 28101

Ambleside Health Centre
Rydal Road, Ambleside, Cumbria LA22 9BP
Tel: 015394 32693

Pharmacists

Seascale

Seascale Pharmacy
Gosforth Road, Seascale, Cumbria CA20 1PR
Tel: 019467 28323

Ambleside

Thomas Bell
Ambleside, Cumbria LA22 0AD
Tel: 015394 33345

Boots
Market Cross, Ambleside, Cumbria LA22 9DR
Tel: 015394 33355

Emergency Services

Procedure

Dial 999
Police, Fire, Ambulance, Coastguard
When asked for location, give name of place clearly and indicate
CUMBRIA
In rural locations give a map reference
For deaf, hearing and speech impaired
Send a Text Message
Text:
Where you are
Why you need help
to 07786 208 999

Police

NON EMERGENCY NUMBER: 0845 33 00 247

Whitehaven
Scotch Street, Whitehaven CA28 7NN
This station is manned 8am – 12 midnight

Ambleside Police Station
Rydal Road, Ambleside, Cumbria LA22 9AY
This station is unmanned.

Weather

Met Office: St. Bees Head
http://www.metoffice.gov.uk/weather/uk/nw/st_bees_head_latest_
weather.html

Local Radio

CFM
http://www.cfmradio.com/
http://www.cfmradio.com/
Whitehaven – 103.4 FM

BBC Radio Cumbria
http://www.bbc.co.uk/cumbria/local_radio/
http://www.bbc.co.uk/cumbria/local_radio/
Frequencies:
North, East and West 95.6 FM
South 96.1 FM
Whitehaven 104.1 FM

Other Useful Bodies

World Owl Trust
The Owl Centre Muncaster Castle Ravenglass Cumbria CA18 1RQ
United Kingdom.
Telephone: 01229 717393
Fax: 01229 717107

The Lake District National Park Authority
Murley Moss, Oxenholme Road, Kendal, Cumbria LA9 7RL
Tel: 01539 724555
Fax: 01539 740822

A selection of Hotels, Pubs along the Route

(Not a definitive list)

Ravenglass

The Pennington Hotel
http://www.penningtonhotels.com/
01229 717222

The Ratty Arms (pub)
01229 717676

Holly House Guest House
01229 717230

Rosegarth
http://www.rose-garth.co.uk/
01229 717275

Bay Horse
http://www.bayhorseravenglass.co.uk/
01229 717250
email:mike.elaine@bayhorseravenglass.co.uk

Walls Caravan Park
http://www.campingandcaravanningclub.co.uk/ukcampsites
Tel: 01229 717250

The Old Butcher's Shop (Shop)
01229 717273

Saltcoats

Saltcoats Caravan Park
01229 717241

Drigg

The Victoria Hotel
Tel: 01946 724231

Spindle Craft (Shop)
Tel: 01946 724335

Muncaster

Muncaster Guest House
http://www.muncastercountryguesthouse.com/
Ravenglass, Cumbria CA18 1RD
Tel: 01229 717693

The Coachmans Quarters
http://www.muncaster.co.uk/
Muncaster Castle, Ravenglass, Cumbria CA18 1RQ
Tel: 01229 717614

Eskdale

The Bower House Inn
http://www.bowerhouseinn.co.uk/

Eskdale, Holmrook, Cumbria, CA19 1TD
Tel: 01946 723 244

Forest Howe B&B
Eskdale Green, Holmrook CA19 1TR
Tel: 019467 23201
email: info@foresthow.co.uk

Randle How B&B
Eskdale Green, Holmrook, Cumbria CA19 1UA
Tel: 019467 23336

Fisherground Farm Campsite
Boot, Holmrook CA19 1TF
Tel: 019467 23349

King George IV
http://www.kinggeorge-eskdale.co.uk/
Eskdale, Cumbria CA19 1TS
Phone: 01946 723262

Boot

Brook House Inn
http://www.brookhouseinn.co.uk
Boot, Eskdale, Cumbria .CA19 1TG
Tel: 019467 23288

The Boot Inn
http://www.bootinn.co.uk
Boot, Eskdale, Cumbria CA19 1TG
Tel. 019467 23224

The Woolpack
Boot, Eskdale, Cumbria CA19 1TH
Tel: 019467 23230
email: enquiries@woolpack.co.uk

YHA
Tel: 0870 7705824
email: eskdale@yha.org.uk

Hollins Campsite
Boot, Holmrook CA19 1TH
Tel: 019467 23253

Dale View B&B
http://www.booteskdale.co.uk
Boot, Eskdale, Cumbria
Tel: 019467 23236

Penny Hill Farm B&B
Boot, Eskdale, Cumbria CA19 1TH
Tel: 019467 23274

Stanley Ghyll House Guest House
Eskdale, Cumbria CA19 1TF
Tel: 019467 23327

Little Langdale

Three Shires Inn
Little Langdale, Ambleside, Cumbria, LA22 9NZ
Tel: 015394 37215
e-mail: enquiry@threeshiresinn.co.uk

Fell Foot Farm
Little Langdale, Ambleside, Cumbria LA22 9PE
Tel: 015394 37149

Great Langdale – Dungeon Ghyll

National Trust Campsite – see National Trust 015394 35353

Old Dungeon Ghyll Hotel
Great Langdale, Ambleside, Cumbria LA22 9JY
Tel: 015394 37272

Skelwith Fold
http://www.holmesheadfarm.co.uk
Holmstead Farm, Skelwith Fold, Ambleside, Cumbria
Tel: 015394 33048

Elterwater Park
http://www.elterwater.com
Skelwith Bridge, Cumbria
Tel: 015394 32227

Skelwith Bridge Hotel
http://www.skelwithbridgehotel.co.uk
Skelwith Bridge, Cumbria
Tel: 015394 32115

Ambleside

Wateredge Inn
Waterhead, Ambleside, Cumbria LA22 0EP
Tel: 015394 32332

Salutation Hotel
Lake Road, Ambleside, Cumbria LA22 9BX
Tel: 015394 32244

Smallwood House Hotel
Compston Road, Ambleside, Cumbria LA22 9DJ
Tel: 015394 32330

Guest Houses (A selection, certainly not definitive)

3 Cambridge Villas
Church Street, Ambleside, Cumbria
Tel: 015394 32307

Highfield
Lake Road, Ambleside, Cumbria
Tel: 015394 32671

Elder Grove
Lake Road, Ambleside, Cumbria
Tel: 015394 32504

Hillsdale
Church Street, Ambleside, Cumbria
Tel: 015394 33174

Old Vicarage
Vicarage Road, Ambleside, Cumbria
Tel: 015394 33364

HOSTELS

Ambleside Backpackers
Old Lake Road, Cumbria
Tel: 015394 32340

YHA Hostel
Ambleside
Tel: 015394 32304

ALL SERVICES

Ambleside Post Office
Central Buildings, Market Cross, Ambleside, Cumbria LA22 9BS
(Monday-Saturday)

Other Useful Information

Ravenglass Post Office
Main Street, Ravenglass CA18 1SG
Tel: 01229 717281

Eskdale Stores
Eskdale Green, Holmrook, Cumbria CA19 1TX
Tel: 019467 23229

Eskdale Post Office
St Bega's Church, Eskdale Green (Mon- Thur)

Boot Post Office
Dale View, Eskdale CA19 1TG (Tues & Thur)

Little Langdale Post Office
Little Langdale, School House, Ambleside, Cumbria LA22 9NY (Thur)

Attractions

Ravenglass & Eskdale Railway
Ravenglass, Cumbria CA18 1SW
Tel: 01229 717171

The Old Butcher's Shop Gift & Craft Centre
Main Street, Ravenglass, Cumbria CA18 1SQ
Tel: 01229 717273

Muncaster Castle
Ravenglass, Cumbria CA18 1RQ
Tel: 01229 717 614

World Owl Trust
The Owl Centre
Muncaster, Cumbria CA18 1RQ
Tel: 01229 717393

Boot Mill
Boot, Eskdale, Cumbria
Tel: 019467 23335

Fell Foot Gallery
Boot, Cumbria CA19 1TG
Tel: 019467 23316

Touchstone Interiors
Skelwith Bridge Cumbria LA22 9NN
Tel: 015394 34002

Chesters Coffee Shop
Skelwith Bridge Cumbria LA22 9NN
Tel: 015394 32553

Zeffirellis (Cinema, Café, Jazz Bar, Restaurant)
Compston Road, Ambleside, Cumbria LA22 9AD
Tel: 015394 33845

Organisations

West Cumbrian habitats

Railway Heritage

Ravenglass & Eskdale Preservation Society
Hon Membership Secretary
Mr P. Taylor
12 Wholehouse Road, Seascale, Cumbria CA20 1QY

Natural England
Juniper House, Murley Moss, Oxenholme Road, Kendal, Cumbria
LA9 7RL

Archaeological Sites Cumbrian coast

English Heritage
Canada House, 3 Chepstow Street, Manchester M1 5FW

Birds of the Cumbrian Coast

RSPB
The Lodge, Sandy, Bedfordshire SG19 2DL

Wildlife of the Cumbrian Coast

Cumbria Wildlife Trust
Plumgarths, Crook Road, Kendal, Cumbria LA8 8LX

Promotion of better facilities for visitors

Hadrian's Wall Heritage Ltd
East Peterel Field, Dipton Mill Road, Hexham, Northumberland
NE46 2JT

Community Archaeology

Hadrian's Wall Country
http://www.hadrians-wall.org

Portal to details of Hadrian's Wall, including Western Frontier

Boot Mill
Eskdale Mill and Heritage Trust,
c/o Bowerbank
Eskdale Green
Cumbria
CA19 1TD

British Museum
http://www.thebritishmuseum.ac.uk

National Health Service
http://www.nhs.uk/Pages/homepage.asp

Cumbria Constabulary
http://www.cumbria.police.uk

Academic Material

Data Regarding Park Head Tile Kilns (Muncaster Head)
Transactions of the Cumberland and Westmorland Antiquarian &
Archaeological Society 60/1960/1-12
Transactions of the Cumberland and Westmorland Antiquarian &
Archaeological Society 61/1961/47-56
The journal of Roman studies 51/1961/164

Data Regarding Park Head Forge Site
Post-medieval archaeology: the journal of the Society for Post-
Medieval Archaeology 2/1968/192
Post-medieval archaeology: the journal of the Society for Post-
Medieval Archaeology 3/1969/207-8

Notes on Galava
Note Royal Commission on Historical Monuments (England)
Westmorland Inventory 1936/1-3
Reference The National Trust annual archaeological review 6/1998
Note Transactions of the Cumberland and Westmorland Antiquarian
& Archaeological Society 14/1914/433
Note Transactions of the Cumberland and Westmorland Antiquarian

Et Archaeological Society 15/1915/1
Note Royal Commission on Historical Monuments (England)
Westmorland Inventory 1936/1-3
Reference The National Trust annual archaeological review 6/1998
Full report Transactions of the Cumberland and Westmorland
Antiquarian Et Archaeological Society 21/1921/1-42

Notes on Muncaster
Braithwaite, J. J. (2004). Magnetic variances associated with 'haunt-type' experiences: A comparison using time-synchronized baseline measurements. *European Journal of Parapsychology,* 19, 3-28.
Braithwaite, J. J., Perez-Aquino, K., Et Townsend, M. (2004). In search of magnetic anomalies associated with haunt-type experiences: Pulses and patterns in dual time-synchronised measurements. *Journal of Parapsychology,* 68, 255-288

Bibliography

Bellhouse R., Roman Sites on the Cumberland Coast: A new schedule of coastal sites, Cumberland & Westmorland Antiquarian & Archaeological Society Research Series, Volume III (1989)

Collingwood R.G & Wright R.P, Roman Inscriptions of Britain, Oxford (1965)

Defoe D, A Tour through the Whole Island of Great Britain, (1726)

Hanson W.S. Hanson & Keppie, L.J.F., Frontier Studies, Oxford (1979)

Higham, N.J. and Jones, G.D.B, Frontier, forts and farmers. Cumbria aerial survey 1974-75. Archaeological Journal 132: 16-53 (1975)

Potter T., Romans in North West England, (1979)

Schubert, H.R., History of the British Iron and Steel Industry (1957). R.F. Tylecote, History of Metallurgy (1991)

Shotter D, Roman Coins from North-West England ,Lancaster (1990)

Tacitus C, Trans. Mattingley H., Revised Hanford S, The Agricola, (1970)

Tyler I, The Gunpowder Mills of Cumbria, Blue Rock Publications, Amadeus Press, Cleckheaton, 2002

Wilson P., Morphology and significance of some Loch Lomond Stadial moraines in the south-central Lake District, England Source: http://www.ingentaconnect.com/content/geol/pga

Proceedings of the Geologists' Association, Volume 113, Number 1, 2002 , pp9-21(13)

Wilson J., Victoria County History 'Houses of Benedictine monks: The priory of St Bees', A History of the County of Cumberland: Volume 2 (1905)

Zeller Van P., Ravenglass: Roman Port to Railway Junction (2001)

Electronic Bibliography

http://www.middelaldercentret.dk/pdf/gunpowder4.pdf

Transactions of the Cumberland and Westmorland Antiquarian & Archaeological Society

Charlesworth, D. The Granaries at Hardknott Castle 63, 1963 Page 148-152

Collingwood, R G, 'The Roman road from Ambleside to Wrynose'. ns, 21, Page 1921, Page 24-9

Fair, M. C. 'A group of remains near Eskdale Green', 38 1938, Page 267-70

Fair, M. C. 'Eskdale notes. The Roman road at Ravenglass'. 26 1926, Page 423-8

Leech, R. H.; Scott, D. (ed.). 'The Roman fort and vicus at Ambleside: archaeological research in 1982', 93, 1993, Page 51-74

McGilchrist, C. R. B. 'The Roman road in Eskdale' 19 1919, Page 17-29

Pugmire, M. 'The Roman road from Ravenglass to Ambleside in Lower Langdale : a suggested surviving fragment'. 3rd ser., 3, 2003, Page 85-89.

Richmond, I.A. 'The Roman road from Ambleside to Ravenglass'. ns, 49, 1949, Page 15-31

Thorley, J. 'The Ambleside Roman gravestone' 3rd ser., 2 , 2002, Page 51-58

Tylecote, R. F.; Cherry, J. 'The 17th century bloomery at Muncaster Head'. ns, 70, 1970, Page 69-109

C&WAAS Research Series

Bellhouse, R., 1989 Roman Sites on the Cumberland Coast: A new schedule of coastal sites, Cumberland & Westmorland Antiquarian & Archaeological Society Research Series, Volume III

Potter, T.W., Romans in north-west England: excavations at the Roman forts of Ravenglass, Watercrook and Bowness on Solway (Cumberland and Westmorland Antiquarian and Archaeological Society, research series, 1). [s.l.]: Cumberland and Westmorland Antiquarian and Archaeological Society, 1979.

Archaeological Journal

Higham, N.J. and Jones, G.D.B., 1975 Frontier, forts and farmers. Cumbria aerial survey 1974-75. Archaeological Journal 132: 16-53

Northern Mine Research Society

Goodchild, John F. 'Dabbling in Eskdale Iron Mining'. British mining, 75 (2004), 36-42. Publisher: Northern Mine Research Society. ISSN 0308-2199

Society for the Promotion of Roman Studies

Welsby, D. A. 'Pottery Production at Muncaster, Eskdale in the Second Century A.D'. Britannia, 16 (1985), 127-40. Publisher: Society for the Promotion of Roman Studies. ISSN 0068113X

Proceedings of the Society of Antiquaries of London
Cowper, H.S. 'Discoveries of the Roman road near Ambleside'.
   Proceedings of the Society of Antiquaries of London, 2nd ser., 18
   (1901), 267-71.

Inscription Translations

Hardknott

"For the emperor Caesar Trajanus Hadrianus Augustus, son of the
   Divine Trajanus Parthicus, grandson of the Divine Nerva, Pontifex
   Maximus, – consul three times, –pro-praetorian legate of the
   emperor, the Fourth Cohort of Delmatians made this."

(RIB 793a; AD119-38; JRS lv 1965, p.222, no.7)

Ambleside (Galava)

"To the good spirits of the departed and Flavius Fuscinus, veteran,
   former ordinarius,[1] he lived for fifty-five years."
(RIB 755.a; primary)

"To the good spirits of the departed and Flavius Romanus, actarius,[2] he
   lived for thirty-five years, (killed) in service whilst standing up to the
   enemy."
(RIB 755.a; secondary)

Both (JRS xliii 1963, p.160, no.4)

Acknowledgements

Thanks to
My wife Susie
John Buckland
The people of Ravenglass, Eskdale, Langdale and Ambleside

...and last, but most certainly not least, our photographer's
"Inferior Combustion Chariot", parked outside Hardknott Fort.